Java Deep Learning Essentials

Dive into the future of data science and learn how to build the sophisticated algorithms that are fundamental to deep learning and AI with Java

Yusuke Sugomori

BIRMINGHAM - MUMBAI

Java Deep Learning Essentials

First published: May 2016

Production reference: 1250516

Published by Packt Publishing Ltd.
Livery Place
35 Livery Street
Birmingham B3 2PB, UK.

ISBN 978-1-78528-219-5

www.packtpub.com

Credits

Author
Yusuke Sugomori

Reviewers
Wei Di
Vikram Kalabi

Commissioning Editor
Kartikey Pandey

Acquisition Editor
Manish Nainani

Content Development Editor
Rohit Singh

Technical Editor
Vivek Arora

Copy Editor
Ameesha Smith Green

Project Coordinator
Izzat Contractor

Proofreader
Safis Editing

Indexer
Mariammal Chettiyar

Graphics
Abhinash Sahu

Production Coordinator
Arvindkumar Gupta

Cover Work
Arvindkumar Gupta

About the Author

Yusuke Sugomori is a creative technologist with a background in information engineering. When he was a graduate school student, he cofounded Gunosy with his colleagues, which uses machine learning and web-based data mining to determine individual users' respective interests and provides an optimized selection of daily news items based on those interests. This algorithm-based app has gained a lot of attention since its release and now has more than 10 million users. The company has been listed on the Tokyo Stock Exchange since April 28, 2015.

In 2013, Sugomori joined Dentsu, the largest advertising company in Japan based on nonconsolidated gross profit in 2014, where he carried out a wide variety of digital advertising, smartphone app development, and big data analysis. He was also featured as one of eight "new generation" creators by the Japanese magazine Web Designing.

In April 2016, he joined a medical start-up as cofounder and CTO.

About the Reviewers

Wei Di is a data scientist. She is passionate about creating smart and scalable analytics and data mining solutions that can impact millions of individuals and empower successful businesses.

Her interests also cover wide areas including artificial intelligence, machine learning, and computer vision. She was previously associated with the eBay Human Language Technology team and eBay Research Labs, with a focus on image understanding for large scale applications and joint learning from both visual and text information. Prior to that, she was with Ancestry.com working on large-scale data mining and machine learning models in the areas of record linkage, search relevance, and ranking. She received her PhD from Purdue University in 2011 with focuses on data mining and image classification.

Vikram Kalabi is a data scientist. He is working on a Cognitive System that can enable smart plant breeding. His work is primarily in predictive analytics and mathematical optimization. He has also worked on large scale data-driven decision making systems with a focus on recommender systems. He is excited about data science that can help improve farmer's life and help reduce food scarcity in the world. He is a certified data scientist from John Hopkins University.

www.PacktPub.com

eBooks, discount offers, and more

Did you know that Packt offers eBook versions of every book published, with PDF and ePub files available? You can upgrade to the eBook version at www.PacktPub.com and as a print book customer, you are entitled to a discount on the eBook copy. Get in touch with us at customercare@packtpub.com for more details.

At www.PacktPub.com, you can also read a collection of free technical articles, sign up for a range of free newsletters and receive exclusive discounts and offers on Packt books and eBooks.

https://www2.packtpub.com/books/subscription/packtlib

Do you need instant solutions to your IT questions? PacktLib is Packt's online digital book library. Here, you can search, access, and read Packt's entire library of books.

Why subscribe?

- Fully searchable across every book published by Packt
- Copy and paste, print, and bookmark content
- On demand and accessible via a web browser

Table of Contents

Preface

With an increasing interest in AI around the world, deep learning has attracted a great deal of public attention. Every day, deep learning algorithms are used across different industries. Deep learning has provided a revolutionary step to actualize AI. While it is a revolutionary technique, deep learning is often thought to be complicated, and so it is often kept from much being known of its contents. Theories and concepts based on deep learning are not complex or difficult. In this book, we'll take a step-by-step approach to learn theories and equations for the correct understanding of deep learning. You will find implementations from scratch, with detailed explanations of the cautionary notes for practical use cases.

What this book covers

Chapter 1, Deep Learning Overview, explores how deep learning has evolved.

Chapter 2, Algorithms for Machine Learning - Preparing for Deep Learning, implements machine learning algorithms related to deep learning.

Chapter 3, Deep Belief Nets and Stacked Denoising Autoencoders, dives into Deep Belief Nets and Stacked Denoising Autoencoders algorithms.

Chapter 4, Dropout and Convolutional Neural Networks, discovers more deep learning algorithms with Dropout and Convolutional Neural Networks.

Chapter 5, Exploring Java Deep Learning Libraries – DL4J, ND4J, and More, gains an insight into the deep learning library, DL4J, and its practical uses.

Chapter 6, Approaches to Practical Applications – Recurrent Neural Networks and More, lets you devise strategies to use deep learning algorithms and libraries in the real world.

Chapter 7, Other Important Deep Learning Libraries, explores deep learning further with Theano, TensorFlow, and Caffe.

Chapter 8, What's Next?, explores recent deep learning movements and events, and looks into useful deep learning resources.

What you need for this book

We'll implement deep learning algorithms using Lambda Expressions, hence Java 8 or above is required. Also, we'll use the Java library DeepLearning4J 0.4 or above.

Who this book is for

This book is for Java developers who want to know about deep learning algorithms and wish to implement them in applications.

Since this book covers the core concepts of and approaches to both machine learning and deep learning, no previous experience in machine learning is required.

Also, we will implement deep learning algorithms with very simple codes, so elementary Java developers will also find this book useful for developing both their Java skills and deep learning skills.

Conventions

In this book, you will find a number of text styles that distinguish between different kinds of information. Here are some examples of these styles and an explanation of their meaning.

Code words in text, database table names, folder names, filenames, file extensions, pathnames, dummy URLs, user input, and Twitter handles are shown as follows: "Let's take a look at CNNMnistExample.java in the package of convolution."

A block of code is set as follows:

```
<dependency>
    <groupId>org.nd4j</groupId>
    <artifactId>nd4j-jcublas-7.0</artifactId>
    <version>${nd4j.version}</version>
</dependency>
```

Any command-line input or output is written as follows:

```
[[7.00,7.00]
 [7.00,7.00]
 [7.00,7.00]]
```

New terms and **important words** are shown in bold. Words that you see on the screen, for example, in menus or dialog boxes, appear in the text like this: "If you're using IntelliJ, you can import the project from **File | New | Project** from existing sources."

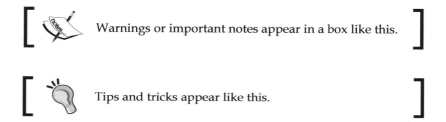

Warnings or important notes appear in a box like this.

Tips and tricks appear like this.

Reader feedback

Feedback from our readers is always welcome. Let us know what you think about this book—what you liked or disliked. Reader feedback is important for us as it helps us develop titles that you will really get the most out of.

To send us general feedback, simply e-mail feedback@packtpub.com, and mention the book's title in the subject of your message.

If there is a topic that you have expertise in and you are interested in either writing or contributing to a book, see our author guide at www.packtpub.com/authors.

Customer support

Now that you are the proud owner of a Packt book, we have a number of things to help you to get the most from your purchase.

Downloading the example code

You can download the example code files for this book from your account at `http://www.packtpub.com`. If you purchased this book elsewhere, you can visit `http://www.packtpub.com/support` and register to have the files e-mailed directly to you.

You can download the code files by following these steps:

1. Log in or register to our website using your e-mail address and password.
2. Hover the mouse pointer on the **SUPPORT** tab at the top.
3. Click on **Code Downloads & Errata**.
4. Enter the name of the book in the **Search** box.
5. Select the book for which you're looking to download the code files.
6. Choose from the drop-down menu where you purchased this book from.
7. Click on **Code Download**.

You can also download the code files by clicking on the **Code Files** button on the book's webpage at the Packt Publishing website. This page can be accessed by entering the book's name in the **Search** box. Please note that you need to be logged in to your Packt account.

Once the file is downloaded, please make sure that you unzip or extract the folder using the latest version of:

- WinRAR / 7-Zip for Windows
- Zipeg / iZip / UnRarX for Mac
- 7-Zip / PeaZip for Linux

The code bundle for the book is also hosted on GitHub at `https://github.com/PacktPublishing/Java-Deep-Learning-Essentials`. We also have other code bundles from our rich catalog of books and videos available at `https://github.com/PacktPublishing/`. Check them out!

Errata

Although we have taken every care to ensure the accuracy of our content, mistakes do happen. If you find a mistake in one of our books—maybe a mistake in the text or the code—we would be grateful if you could report this to us. By doing so, you can save other readers from frustration and help us improve subsequent versions of this book. If you find any errata, please report them by visiting http://www.packtpub.com/submit-errata, selecting your book, clicking on the **Errata Submission Form** link, and entering the details of your errata. Once your errata are verified, your submission will be accepted and the errata will be uploaded to our website or added to any list of existing errata under the Errata section of that title.

To view the previously submitted errata, go to https://www.packtpub.com/books/content/support and enter the name of the book in the search field. The required information will appear under the **Errata** section.

Piracy

Piracy of copyrighted material on the Internet is an ongoing problem across all media. At Packt, we take the protection of our copyright and licenses very seriously. If you come across any illegal copies of our works in any form on the Internet, please provide us with the location address or website name immediately so that we can pursue a remedy.

Please contact us at copyright@packtpub.com with a link to the suspected pirated material.

We appreciate your help in protecting our authors and our ability to bring you valuable content.

Questions

If you have a problem with any aspect of this book, you can contact us at questions@packtpub.com, and we will do our best to address the problem.

Deep Learning Overview

Artificial Intelligence (AI) is a word that you might start to see more often these days. AI has become a hot topic not only in academic society, but also in the field of business. Large tech companies such as Google and Facebook have actively bought AI-related start-ups. Mergers and acquisitions in these AI areas have been especially active, with big money flowing into AI. The Japanese IT/mobile carrier company Softbank released a robot called Pepper in June 2014, which understands human feelings, and a year later they have started to sell Pepper to general consumers. This is a good movement for the field of AI, without a doubt.

The idea of AI has been with us for decades. So, why has AI suddenly became a hot field? One of the factors that has driven recent AI-related movements, and is almost always used with the word AI, is **deep learning**. After deep learning made a vivid debut and its technological capabilities began to grow exponentially, people started to think that finally AI would become a reality. It sounds like deep learning is definitely something we need to know. So, what exactly is it?

To answer the previous questions, in this chapter we'll look at why and how AI has become popular by following its history and fields of studies. The topics covered will be:

- The former approaches and techniques of AI
- An introduction to machine learning and a look at how it has evolved into deep learning
- An introduction to deep learning and some recent use cases

If you already know what deep learning is or if you would like to find out about the specific algorithm of the deep learning/implementation technique, you can skip this chapter and jump directly to *Chapter 2, Algorithms for Machine Learning – Preparing for Deep Learning*.

Although deep learning is an innovative technique, it is not actually that complicated. It is rather surprisingly simple. Reading through this book, you will see how brilliant it is. I sincerely hope that this book will contribute to your understanding of deep learning and thus to your research and business.

Transition of AI

So, why is it now that deep learning is in the spotlight? You might raise this question, especially if you are familiar with machine learning, because deep learning is not that different to any other machine learning algorithm (don't worry if you don't know this, as we'll go through it later in the book). In fact, we can say that deep learning is the adaptation of neural networks, one of the algorithms of machine learning, which mimics the structure of a human brain. However, what deep learning can achieve is much more significant and different to any other machine learning algorithm, including neural networks. If you see what processes and research deep learning has gone through, you will have a better understanding of deep learning itself. So, let's go through the transition of AI. You can just skim through this while sipping your coffee.

Definition of AI

All of a sudden, AI has become a hot topic in the world; however, as it turns out, actual AI doesn't exist yet. Of course, research is making progress in creating actual AI, but it will take more time to achieve it. Pleased or not, the human brain—which could be called "intelligence"—is structured in an extremely complicated way and you can't easily replicate it.

But wait a moment - we see many advertisements for products with the phrase *by AI* or *using AI* all over them. Are they fraudulent? Actually, they are! Surprised? You might see words like *recommendation system by AI* or *products driven by AI*, but the word *AI* used here doesn't indicate the actual meaning of AI. Strictly speaking, the word AI is used with a much broader meaning. The research into AI and the AI techniques accumulated in the past have achieved only some parts of AI, but now people are using the word AI for those parts too.

Let's look at a few examples. Roughly divided, there are three different categories recognized as AI in general:

- Simple repetitive machine movements that a human programmed beforehand. For example, high speed processing industrial robots that only process the same set of work.
- Searching or guessing answers to a given assignment following rules set by a human. For example, the iRobot Roomba can clean up along the shape of a room as it can assume the shape of a room by bumping into obstacles.

- Providing an answer to unknown data by finding measurable regularity from the existing data. For example, a product recommendation system based on a user's purchase history or distributing banner ads among ad networks falls under this category.

People use the word AI for these categories and, needless to say, new technology that utilizes deep learning is also called AI. Yet, these technologies are different both in structure and in what they can do. So, which should we specifically call AI? Unfortunately, people have different opinions about that question and the answer cannot be objectively explained. Academically, a term has been set as either **strong AI** or **weak AI** depending on the level that a machine can achieve. However, in this book, to avoid confusion, AI is used to mean (*Not yet achieved*) *human-like intelligence that is hard to distinguish from the actual human brain*. The field of AI is being drastically developed, and the possibility of AI becoming reality is exponentially higher when driven by deep learning. This field is booming now more than ever in history. How long this boom will continue depends on future research.

AI booms in the past

AI suddenly became a hot topic recently: however, this is not the first AI boom. When you look back to the past, research into AI has been conducted for decades and there has been a cycle of being active and inactive. The recent boom is the third boom. Therefore, some people actually think that, at this time, it's just an evanescent boom again.

However, the latest boom has a significant difference from the past booms. Yes, that is deep learning. Deep learning has achieved what the past techniques could not achieve. What is that? Simply put, a machine itself is able to find out the feature quantity from the given data, and learn. With this achievement, we can see the great possibility of AI becoming a reality, because until now a machine couldn't understand a new concept by itself and a human needed to input a certain feature quantity in advance using past techniques created in the AI field.

It doesn't look like a huge difference if you just read this fact, but there's a world of difference. There has been a long path taken before reaching the stage where a machine can measure feature quantity by itself. People were finally able to take a big step forward when a machine could obtain intelligence driven by deep learning. So, what's the big difference between the past techniques and deep learning? Let's briefly look back into the past AI field to get a better sense of the difference.

The first AI boom came in the late 1950s. Back then, the mainstream research and development of a search program was based on fixed rules—needless to say, they were human-defined. The search was, simply put, dividing cases. In this search, if we wanted a machine to perform any process, we had to write out every possible pattern we might need for the process. A machine can calculate much faster than a human can. It doesn't matter how enormous the patterns are, a machine can easily handle them. A machine will keep searching a million times and eventually will find the best answer. However, even if a machine can calculate at high speed, if it is just searching for an answer randomly and blindly it will take a massive amount of time. Yes, don't forget that constraint condition, "time." Therefore, further studies were conducted on how to make the search more efficient. The most popular search methods among the studies were **depth-first search (DFS)** and **breadth-first search (BFS)**.

Out of every possible pattern you can think of, search for the most efficient path and make the best possible choice among them within a realistic time frame. By doing this, you should get the best answer each time. Based on this hypothesis, two searching or traversing algorithms for a tree of graph data structures were developed: DFS and BFS. Both start at the root of a graph or tree, and DFS explores as far as possible along each branch before backtracking, whereas BFS explores the neighbor nodes first before moving to the next level neighbors. Here are some example diagrams that show the difference between DFS and BFS:

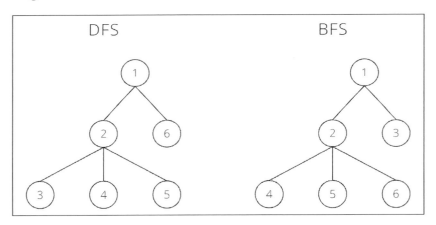

These search algorithms could achieve certain results in a specific field, especially fields like Chess and Shogi. This board game field is one of the areas that a machine excels in. If it is given an input of massive amounts of win/lose patterns, past game data, and all the permitted moves of a piece in advance, a machine can evaluate the board position and decide the best possible next move from a very large range of patterns.

For those of you who are interested in this field, let's look into how a machine plays chess in more detail. Let's say a machine makes the first move as "white," and there are 20 possible moves for both "white" and "black" for the next move. Remember the tree-like model in the preceding diagram. From the top of the tree at the start of the game, there are 20 branches underneath as white's next possible move. Under one of these 20 branches, there's another 20 branches underneath as black's next possible movement, and so on. In this case, the tree has $20 \times 20 = 400$ branches for black, depending on how white moves, $400 \times 20 = 8,000$ branches for white, $8,000 \times 20 = 160,000$ branches again for black, and... feel free to calculate this if you like.

A machine generates this tree and evaluates every possible board position from these branches, deciding the best arrangement in a second. How deep it goes (how many levels of the tree it generates and evaluates) is controlled by the speed of the machine. Of course, each different piece's movement should also be considered and embedded in a program, so the chess program is not as simple as previously thought, but we won't go into detail about this in this book. As you can see, it's not surprising that a machine can beat a human at Chess. A machine can evaluate and calculate massive amounts of patterns at the same time, in a much shorter time than a human could. It's not a new story that a machine has beaten a Chess champion; a machine has won a game over a human. Because of stories like this, people expected that AI would become a true story.

Unfortunately, reality is not that easy. We then found out that there was a big wall in front of us preventing us from applying the search algorithm to reality. Reality is, as you know, complicated. A machine is good at processing things at high speed based on a given set of rules, but it cannot find out how to act and what rules to apply by itself when only a task is given. Humans unconsciously evaluate, discard many things/options that are not related to them, and make a choice from millions of things (patterns) in the real world whenever they act. A machine cannot make these unconscious decisions like humans can. If we create a machine that can appropriately consider a phenomenon that happens in the real world, we can assume two possibilities:

- A machine tries to accomplish its task or purpose without taking into account secondarily occurring incidents and possibilities
- A machine tries to accomplish its task or purpose without taking into account irrelevant incidents and possibilities

Both of these machines would still freeze and be lost in processing before they accomplished their purpose when humans give them a task; in particular, the latter machine would immediately freeze before even taking its first action. This is because these elements are almost infinite and a machine can't sort them out within a realistic time if it tries to think/search these infinite patterns. This issue is recognized as one of the important challenges in the AI field, and it's called the **frame problem**.

A machine can achieve great success in the field of Chess or Shogi because the searching space, the space a machine should be processing within, is limited (set in a certain frame) in advance. You can't write out an enormous amount of patterns, so you can't define what the best solution is. Even if you are forced to limit the number of patterns or to define an optimal solution, you can't get the result within an economical time frame for use due to the enormous amounts of calculation needed. After all, the research at that time would only make a machine follow detailed rules set by a human. As such, although this search method could succeed in a specific area, it is far from achieving actual AI. Therefore, the first AI boom cooled down rapidly with disappointment.

The first AI boom was swept away; however, on the side, the research into AI continued. The second AI boom came in the 1980s. This time, the movement of so-called **Knowledge Representation (KR)** was booming. KR intended to describe knowledge that a machine could easily understand. If all the knowledge in the world was integrated into a machine and a machine could understand this knowledge, it should be able to provide the right answer even if it is given a complex task. Based on this assumption, various methods were developed for designing knowledge for a machine to understand better. For example, the structured forms on a web page — the semantic web — is one example of an approach that tried to design in order for a machine to understand information easier. An example of how the semantic web is described with KR is shown here:

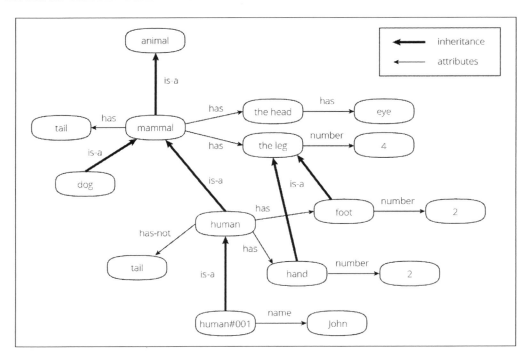

Making a machine gain knowledge is not like a human ordering a machine what to do one-sidedly, but more like a machine being able to respond to what humans ask and then answer. One of the simple examples of how this is applied to the actual world is positive-negative analysis, one of the topics of sentiment analysis. If you input data that defines a tone of positive or negative for every word in a sentence (called "a dictionary") into a machine beforehand, a machine can compare the sentence and the dictionary to find out whether the sentence is positive or negative.

This technique is used for the positive-negative analysis of posts or comments on a social network or blog. If you ask a machine "Is the reaction to this blog post positive or negative?" it analyzes the comments based on its knowledge (dictionary) and replies to you. From the first AI boom, where a machine only followed rules that humans set, the second AI boom showed some progress.

By integrating knowledge into a machine, a machine becomes the almighty. This idea itself is not bad for achieving AI; however, there were two high walls ahead of us in achieving it. First, as you may have noticed, inputting all real-world knowledge requires an almost infinite amount of work now that the Internet is more commonly used and we can obtain enormous amounts of open data from the Web. Back then, it wasn't realistic to collect millions of pieces of data and then analyze and input that knowledge into a machine. Actually, this work of databasing all the world's data has continued and is known as **Cyc** (http://www.cyc.com/). Cyc's ultimate purpose is to build an inference engine based on the database of this knowledge, called **knowledge base**. Here is an example of KR using the Cyc project:

```
(#$isa #$BarackObama #$UnitedStatesPresident)
    "Barack Obama belongs to the collection of U.S. presidents."

(#$genls #$Tree-ThePlant #$Plant)
                                    "All trees are plants."

(#$capitalCity #$Japan #$Tokyo)
                            "Tokyo is the capital of Japan."
```

Second, it's not that a machine understands the actual meaning of the knowledge. Even if the knowledge is structured and systemized, a machine understands it as a mark and never understands the concept. After all, the knowledge is input by a human and what a machine does is just compare the data and assume meaning based on the dictionary. For example, if you know the concept of "apple" and "green" and are taught "green apple = apple + green", then you can understand that "a green apple is a green colored apple" at first sight, whereas a machine can't. This is called the **symbol grounding problem** and is considered one of the biggest problems in the AI field, as well as the frame problem.

The idea was not bad—it did improve AI—however, this approach won't achieve AI in reality as it's not able to create AI. Thus, the second AI boom cooled down imperceptibly, and with a loss of expectation from AI, the number of people who talked about AI decreased. When it came to the question of "Are we really able to achieve AI?" the number of people who answered "no" increased gradually.

Machine learning evolves

While people had a hard time trying to establish a method to achieve AI, a completely different approach had steadily built a generic technology . That approach is called machine learning. You should have heard the name if you have touched on data mining even a little. Machine learning is a strong tool compared to past AI approaches, which simply searched or assumed based on the knowledge given by a human, as mentioned earlier in the chapter, so machine learning is very advanced. Until machine learning, a machine could only search for an answer from the data that had already been inputted. The focus was on how fast a machine could pull out knowledge related to a question from its saved knowledge. Hence, a machine can quickly reply to a question it already knows, but gets stuck when it faces questions it doesn't know.

On the other hand, in machine learning, a machine is literally learning. A machine can cope with unknown questions based on the knowledge it has learned. So, how was a machine able to learn, you ask? What exactly is *learning* here? Simply put, learning is when a machine can divide a problem into "yes" or "no." We'll go through more detail on this in the next chapter, but for now we can say that machine learning is a method of pattern recognition.

We could say that, ultimately, every question in the world can be replaced with a question that can be answered with yes or no. For example, the question "What color do you like?" can be considered almost the same as asking "Do you like red? Do you like green? Do you like blue? Do you like yellow?..." In machine learning, using the ability to calculate and the capacity to process at high speed as a weapon, a machine utilizes a substantial amount of training data, replaces complex questions with yes/no questions, and finds out the regularity with which data is yes, and which data is no (in other words, it learns). Then, with that learning, a machine assumes whether the newly-given data is yes or no and provides an answer. To sum up, machine learning can give an answer by recognizing and sorting out patterns from the data provided and then classifying that data into the possible appropriate pattern (predicting) when it faces unknown data as a question.

In fact, this approach is not doing something especially difficult. Humans also unconsciously classify data into patterns. For example, if you meet a man/woman who's perfectly your type at a party, you might be desperate to know whether the man/woman in front of you has similar feelings towards you. In your head, you would compare his/her way of talking, looks, expressions, or gestures to past experience (that is, data) and assume whether you will go on a date! This is the same as a presumption based on pattern recognition.

Machine learning is a method that can process this pattern recognition not by humans but by a machine in a mechanical manner. So, how can a machine recognize patterns and classify them? The standard of classification by machine learning is a presumption based on a numerical formula called the **probabilistic statistical model**. This approach has been studied based on various mathematical models.

Learning, in other words, is tuning the parameters of a model and, once the learning is done, building a model with one adjusted parameter. The machine then categorizes unknown data into the most possible pattern (that is, the pattern that fits best). Categorizing data mathematically has great merit. While it is almost impossible for a human to process multi-dimensional data or multiple-patterned data, machine learning can process the categorization with almost the same numerical formulas. A machine just needs to add a vector or the number of dimensions of a matrix. (Internally, when it classifies multi-dimensions, it's not done by a classified line or a classified curve but by a hyperplane.)

Until this approach was developed, machines were helpless in terms of responding to unknown data without a human's help, but with machine learning machines became capable of responding to data that humans can't process. Researchers were excited about the possibilities of machine learning and jumped on the opportunity to start working on improving the method. The concept of machine learning itself has a long history, but researchers couldn't do much research and prove the usefulness of machine learning due to a lack of available data. Recently, however, many open-source data have become available online and researchers can easily experiment with their algorithms using the data. Then, the third AI boom came about like this. The environment surrounding machine learning also gave its progress a boost. Machine learning needs a massive amount of data before it can correctly recognize patterns. In addition, it needs to have the capability to process data. The more data and types of patterns it handles, the more the amount of data and the number of calculations increases. Hence, obviously, past technology wouldn't have been able to deal with machine learning.

However, time is progressing, not to mention that the processing capability of machines has improved. In addition, the web has developed and the Internet is spreading all over the world, so open data has increased. With this development, everyone can handle data mining only if they pull data from the web. The environment is set for everyone to casually study machine learning. The web is a treasure box of text-data. By making good use of this text-data in the field of machine learning, we are seeing great development, especially with statistical natural language processing. Machine learning has also made outstanding achievements in the field of image recognition and voice recognition, and researchers have been working on finding the method with the best precision.

Machine learning is utilized in various parts of the business world as well. In the field of natural language processing, the prediction conversion in the **input method editor (IME)** could soon be on your mind. The fields of image recognition, voice recognition, image search, and voice search in the search engine are good examples. Of course, it's not limited to these fields. It is also applied to a wide range of fields from marketing targeting, such as the sales prediction of specific products or the optimization of advertisements, or designing store shelf or space planning based on predicting human behavior, to predicting the movements of the financial market. It can be said that the most used method of data mining in the business world is now machine learning. Yes, machine learning is that powerful. At present, if you hear the word "AI," it's usually the case that the word simply indicates a process done by machine learning.

What even machine learning cannot do

A machine learns by gathering data and predicting an answer. Indeed, machine learning is very useful. Thanks to machine learning, questions that are difficult for a human to solve within a realistic time frame (such as using a 100-dimensional hyperplane for categorization!) are easy for a machine. Recently, "big data" has been used as a buzzword and, by the way, analyzing this big data is mainly done using machine learning too.

Unfortunately, however, even machine learning cannot make AI. From the perspective of "can it actually achieve AI?" machine learning has a big weak point. There is one big difference in the process of learning between machine learning and human learning. You might have noticed the difference, but let's see. Machine learning is the technique of pattern classification and prediction based on input data. If so, what exactly is that input data? Can it use any data? Of course... it can't. It's obvious that it can't correctly predict based on irrelevant data. For a machine to learn correctly, it needs to have appropriate data, but then a problem occurs. A machine is not able to sort out what is appropriate data and what is not. Only if it has the right data can machine learning find a pattern. No matter how easy or difficult a question is, it's humans that need to find the right data.

Let's think about this question: "Is the object in front of you a human or a cat?" For a human, the answer is all too obvious. It's not difficult at all to distinguish them. Now, let's do the same thing with machine learning. First, we need to prepare the format that a machine can read, in other words, we need to prepare the image data of a human and a cat respectively. This isn't anything special. The problem is the next step. You probably just want to use the image data for inputting, but this doesn't work. As mentioned earlier, a machine can't find out what to learn from data by itself. Things a machine should learn need to be processed from the original image data and created by a human. Let's say, in this example, we might need to use data that can define the differences such as face colors, facial part position, the facial outlines of a human and a cat, and so on, as input data. These values, given as inputs that humans need to find out, are called the features.

Machine learning can't do feature engineering. This is the weakest point of machine learning. Features are, namely, variables in the model of machine learning. As this value shows the feature of the object quantitatively, a machine can appropriately handle pattern recognition. In other words, how you set the value of identities will make a huge difference in terms of the precision of prediction. Potentially, there are two types of limitations with machine learning:

- An algorithm can only work well on data with the assumption of the training data - with data that has different distribution. In many cases, the learned model does not generalize well.
- Even the well-trained model lacks the ability to make a smart meta-decision. Therefore, in most cases, machine learning can be very successful in a very narrow direction.

Let's look at a simple example so that you can easily imagine how identities have a big influence on the prediction precision of a model. Imagine there is a corporation that wants to promote a package of asset management based on the amount of assets. The corporation would like to recommend an appropriate product, but as it can't ask a personal question, it needs to predict how many assets a customer might have and prepare in advance. In this case, what type of potential customers shall we consider as an identity? We can assume many factors such as their height, weight, age, address, and so on as an identity, but clearly age or residence seem more relevant than height or weight. You probably won't get a good result if you try machine learning based on height or weight, as it predicts based on irrelevant data, meaning it's just a random prediction.

As such, machine learning can provide an appropriate answer against the question only after the machine reads an appropriate identity. But, unfortunately, the machine can't judge what the appropriate identity is, and the precision of machine learning depends on this feature engineering!

Machine learning has various methods, but the problem of being unable to do feature engineering is seen across all of these. Various methods have been developed and people compete against their precision rates, but after we have achieved precision to a certain extent, people decide whether a method of machine learning is good or bad based on how great a feature they can find. This is no longer a difference in algorithms, but more like a human's intuition or taste, or the fine-tuning of parameters, and this can't be said to be innovative at all. Various methods have been developed, but after all, the hardest thing is to think of the best identity and a human has to do that part anyway.

Things dividing a machine and human

We have gone through three problems: the frame problem, the symbol grounding problem, and feature engineering. None of these problems concern humans at all. So, why can't a machine handle these problems? Let's review the three problems again. If you think about it carefully, you will find that all three problems confront the same issue in the end:

- The frame problem is that a machine can't recognize what knowledge it should use when it is assigned a task

- The symbol grounding problem is that a machine can't understand a concept that puts knowledge together because it only recognizes knowledge as a mark

- The problem of feature engineering in machine learning is that a machine can't find out what the feature is for objects

These problems can be solved only if a machine can sort out *which feature of things/ phenomena it should focus on and what information it should use.* After all, this is the biggest difference between a machine and a human. Every object in this world has its own inherent features. A human is good at catching these features. Is this by experience or by instinct? Anyhow, humans know features, and, based on these features, humans can understand a thing as a "concept."

Now, let's briefly explain what a concept is. First of all, as a premise, take into account that every single thing in this world is constituted of a set of symbol representations and the symbols' content. For example, if you don't know the word "cat" and see a cat when you walk down a street, does it mean you can't recognize a cat? No, this is not true. You know it exists, and if you see another cat just after, you will understand it as "a similar thing to what I saw earlier." Later, you are told "That is called a cat", or you look it up for yourself, and for the first time you can connect the existence and the word.

This word, cat, is the **symbol representation** and the concept that you recognize as a cat is the **symbol content**. You can see these are two sides of the same coin. (Interestingly, there is no necessity between these two sides. There is no necessity to write cat as C-A-T or to pronounce it as such. Even so, in our system of understanding, these are considered to be inevitable. If people hear "cat", we all imagine the same thing.) The concept is, namely, symbol content. These two concepts have terms. The former is called **signifiant** and the latter is called **signifié**, and a set of these two as a pair is called **signe**. (These words are French. You can say signifier, signified, and sign in English, respectively.) We could say what divides a machine and human is whether it can get signifié by itself or not.

What would happen if a machine could find the notable feature from given data? As for the frame problem, if a machine could extract the notable feature from the given data and perform the knowledge representation, it wouldn't have the problem of freezing when thinking of how to pick up the necessary knowledge anymore. In terms of the symbol grounding problem, if a machine could find the feature by itself and understand the concept from the feature, it could understand the inputted symbol.

Needless to say, the feature engineering problem in machine learning would also be solved. If a machine can obtain appropriate knowledge by itself following a situation or a purpose, and not use knowledge from a fixed situation, we can solve the various problems we have been facing in achieving AI. Now, the method that a machine can use to find the important feature value from the given data is close to being accomplished. Yes, finally, this is deep learning. In the next section, I'll explain this deep learning, which is considered to be the biggest breakthrough in the more-than-50 years of AI history.

AI and deep learning

Machine learning, the spark for the third AI boom, is very useful and powerful as a data mining method; however, even with this approach of machine learning, it appeared that the way towards achieving AI was closed. Finding features is a human's role, and here there is a big wall preventing machine learning from reaching AI. It looked like the third AI boom would come to an end as well. However, surprisingly enough, the boom never ended, and on the contrary a new wave has risen. What triggered this wave is deep learning.

With the advent of deep learning, at least in the fields of image recognition and voice recognition, a machine became able to obtain "what should it decide to be a feature value" from the inputted data by itself rather than from a human. A machine that could only handle a symbol as a symbol notation has become able to obtain concepts.

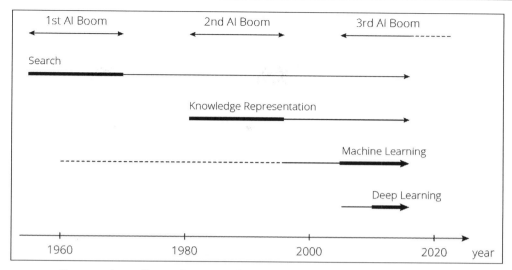

Correspondence diagram between AI booms up to now and the research fields of AI

The first time deep learning appeared was actually quite a while ago, back in 2006. Professor Hinton at Toronto University in Canada, and others, published a paper (https://www.cs.toronto.edu/~hinton/absps/fastnc.pdf). In this paper, a method called **deep belief nets (DBN)** was presented, which is an expansion of neural networks, a method of machine learning. DBN was tested using the **MNIST** database, the standard database for comparing the precision and accuracy of each image recognition method. This database includes 70,000 28 x 28 pixel hand-written character image data of numbers from 0 to 9 (60,000 are for training and 10,000 are for testing).

Then, they constructed a prediction model based on the training data and measured its accuracy based on whether a machine could correctly answer which number from 0 to 9 was written in the test case. Although this paper presented a result with considerably higher precision than a conventional method, it didn't attract much attention at the time, maybe because it was compared with another general method of machine learning.

Then, a while later in 2012, the whole AI research world was shocked by one method. At the world competition for image recognition, **Imagenet Large Scale Visual Recognition Challenge (ILSVRC)**, a method using deep learning called SuperVision (strictly, that's the name of the team), which was developed by Professor Hinton and others from Toronto University, won the competition. It far surpassed the other competitors, with formidable precision. At this competition, the task was assigned for a machine to automatically distinguish whether an image was a cat, a dog, a bird, a car, a boat, and so on. 10 million images were provided as learning data and 150,000 images were used for the test. In this test, each method competes to return the lowest error rate (that is, the highest accuracy rate).

Let's look at the following table that shows the result of the competition:

Rank	Team name	Error
1	SuperVision	0.15315
2	SuperVision	0.16422
3	ISI	0.26172
4	ISI	0.26602
5	ISI	0.26646
6	ISI	0.26952
7	OXFORD_VGG	0.26979
8	XRCE/INRIA	0.27058

You can see that the difference in the error rate between SuperVision and the second position, ISI, is more than 10%. After the second position, it's just a competition within 0.1%. Now you know how greatly SuperVision outshone the others with precision rates. Moreover, surprisingly, it was the first time SuperVision joined this ILSVRC, in other words, image recognition is not their usual field. Until SuperVision (deep learning) appeared, the normal approach for the field of image recognition was machine learning. And, as mentioned earlier, a feature value necessary to use machine learning had to be set or designed by humans. They reiterated design features based on human intuition and experiences and fine-tuning parameters over and over, which, in the end, contributed to improving precision by just 0.1%. The main issue of the research and the competition before deep learning evolved was who was able to invent good feature engineering. Therefore, researchers must have been surprised when deep learning suddenly showed up out of the blue.

There is one other major event that spread deep learning across the world. That event happened in 2012, the same year the world was shocked by SuperVision at ILSVRC, when Google announced that a machine could automatically detect a cat using YouTube videos as learning data from the deep learning algorithm that Google proposed. The details of this algorithm are explained at `http://googleblog.` `blogspot.com/2012/06/using-large-scale-brain-simulations-for.html`. This algorithm extracted 10 million images from YouTube videos and used them as input data. Now, remember, in machine learning, a human has to detect feature values from images and process data. On the other hand, in deep learning, original images can be used for inputs as they are. This shows that a machine itself comes to find features automatically from training data. In this research, a machine learned the concept of a cat. (Only this cat story is famous, but the research was also done with human images and it went well. A machine learned what a human is!) The following image introduced in the research illustrates the characteristics of what deep learning thinks a cat is, after being trained using still frames from unlabeled YouTube videos:

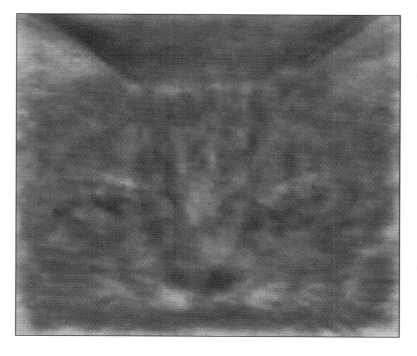

These two big events impressed us with deep learning and triggered the boom that is still accelerating now.

Following the development of the method that can recognize a cat, Google conducted another experiment for a machine to draw a picture by utilizing deep learning. This method is called **Inceptionism** (http://googleresearch.blogspot. ch/2015/06/inceptionism-going-deeper-into-neural.html). As written in the article, in this method, the network is asked:

> *"Whatever you see there, I want more of it!". This creates a feedback loop: if a cloud looks a little bit like a bird, the network will make it look more like a bird. This in turn will make the network recognize the bird even more strongly on the next pass and so forth, until a highly detailed bird appears, seemingly out of nowhere.*

While the use of neural networks in machine learning is a method usually used to detect patterns to be able to specify an image, what Inceptionism does is the opposite. As you can see from the following examples of Inceptionism, these paintings look odd and like the world of a nightmare:

Or rather, they could look artistic. The tool that enables anyone to try Inceptionism is open to the public on GitHub and is named Deep Dream (https://github.com/ google/deepdream). Example implementations are available on that page. You can try them if you can write Python codes.

Well, nothing stops deep learning gaining momentum, but there are still questions, such as what exactly is innovative about deep learning? What special function dramatically increased this precision? Surprisingly, actually, there isn't a lot of difference for deep learning in algorithms. As mentioned briefly, deep learning is an application of neural networks, which is an algorithm of machine learning that imitates the structure of a human brain; nevertheless, a device adopted it and changed everything. The representatives are **pretraining** and **dropout** (with an activation function). These are also keywords for implementation, so please remember them.

To begin with, what does the *deep* in deep learning indicate? As you probably know, the human brain is a circuit structure, and that structure is really complicated. It is made up of an intricate circuit piled up in many layers. On the other hand, when the neural network algorithm first appeared its structure was quite simple. It was a simplified structure of the human brain and the network only had a few layers. Hence, the patterns it could recognize were extremely limited. So, everyone wondered "Can we just accumulate networks like the human brain and make its implementation complex?" Of course, though this approach had already been tried. Unfortunately, as a result, the precision was actually lower than if we had just piled up the networks. Indeed, we faced various issues that didn't occur with a simple network. Why was this? Well, in a human brain, a signal runs into a different part of the circuit depending on what you see. Based on the patterns that differ based on which part of the circuit is stimulated, you can distinguish various things.

To reproduce this mechanism, the neural network algorithm substitutes the linkage of the network by weighting with numbers. This is a great way to do it, but soon a problem occurs. If a network is simple, weights are properly allocated from the learning data and the network can recognize and classify patterns well. However, once a network gets complicated, the linkage becomes too dense and it is difficult to make a difference in the weights. In short, it cannot divide into patterns properly. Also, in a neural network, the network can make a proper model by adopting a mechanism that feeds back errors that occurred during training to the whole network. Again, if the network is simple the feedback can be reflected properly, but if the network has many layers a problem occurs in which the error disappears before it's reflected to the whole network—just imagine if that error was stretched out and diluted.

The intention that things would go well if the network was built with a complicated structure ended in disappointing failure. The concept of the algorithm itself was splendid but it couldn't be called a good algorithm by any standards; that was the world's understanding. While deep learning succeeded in making a network multi-layered, that is, making a network "deep," the key to success was to make each layer learn in stages. The previous algorithm treated the whole multi-layered network as one gigantic neural network and made it learn as one, which caused the problems mentioned earlier.

Hence, deep learning took the approach of making each layer learn in advance. This is literally known as pretraining. In pretraining, learning starts from the lower-dimension layer in order. Then, the data that is learned in the lower layer is treated as input data for the next layer. This way, machines become able to take a step by learning a feature of a low layer at the low-grade layer and gradually learning a feature of a higher grade. For example, when learning what a cat is, the first layer is an outline, the next layer is the shape of its eyes and nose, the next layer is a picture of a face, the next layers is the detail of a face, and so on. Similarly, it can be said that humans take the same learning steps as they catch the whole picture first and see the detailed features later. As each layer learns in stages, the feedback for an error of learning can also be done properly in each layer. This leads to an improvement in precision. There is also a device for each respective approach to each layer's learning, but this will be introduced later on.

We have also addressed the fact that the network became too dense. The method that prevents this density problem is called the **dropout**. Networks with the dropout learn by cutting some linkages randomly within the units of networks. The dropout physically makes the network sparse. Which linkage is cut is random, so a different network is formed at each learning step. Just by looking, you might doubt that this will work, but it greatly contributes to improving the precision and as a result it increases the robustness of the network. The circuit of the human brain also has different places in which to react or not depending on the subject it sees. The dropout seems to be able to successfully imitate this mechanism. By embedding the dropout in the algorithm, the adjustment of the network weight was done well.

Deep learning has seen great success in various fields; however, of course deep learning has a demerit too. As is shown in the name "deep learning," the learning in this method is very deep. This means the steps to complete the learning take a long time. The amount of calculation in this process tends to be enormous. In fact, the previously mentioned learning of the recognition of a cat by Google took three days to be processed with 1,000 computers. Conversely, although the idea of deep learning itself could be conceived using past techniques, it couldn't be implemented. The method wouldn't appear if you couldn't easily use a machine that has a large-scale processing capacity with massive data.

As we keep saying, deep learning is just the first step for a machine to obtain human-like knowledge. Nobody knows what kind of innovation will happen in the future. Yet we can predict to what extent a computer's performance will be improved in the future. To predict this, Moore's law is used. The performance of an integrated circuit that supports the progress of a computer is indicated by the loaded number of transistors. Moore's law shows the number, and the number of transistors is said to double every one and a half years. In fact, the number of transistors in the CPU of a computer has been increasing following Moore's law. Compared to the world's first micro-processor, the Intel® 4004 processor, which had 1x103 (one thousand) transistors, the recent 2015 version, the 5th Generation Intel® Core™ Processor, has 1x109 (one billion)! If this technique keeps improving at this pace, the number of transistors will exceed ten billion, which is more than the number of cells in the human cerebrum.

Based on Moore's law, further in the future in 2045, it is said that we will reach a critical point called **Technical Singularity** where humans will be able to do technology forecasting. By that time, a machine is expected to be able to produce self-recursive intelligence. In other words, in about 30 years, AI will be ready. What will the world be like then…

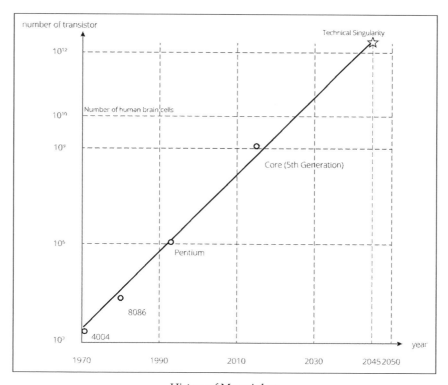

History of Moore's law

The number of transistors loaded in the processor invented by Intel has been increasing smoothly following Moore's law.

The world famous professor Stephen Hawking answered in an interview by the BBC (http://www.bbc.com/news/technology-30290540):

> *"The development of full artificial intelligence could spell the end of the human race."*

Will deep learning become a black magic? Indeed, the progress of technology has sometimes caused tragedy. Achieving AI is still far in the future, yet we should be careful when working on deep learning.

Summary

In this chapter, you learned how techniques in the field of AI have evolved into deep learning. We now know that there were two booms in AI and that we are now in the third boom. Searching and traversing algorithms were developed in the first boom, such as DFS and BFS. Then, the study focused on how knowledge could be represented with symbols that a machine could easily understand in the second boom.

Although these booms had faded away, techniques developed during those times built up much useful knowledge of AI fields. The third boom spread out with machine learning algorithms in the beginning with those of pattern recognition and classification based on probabilistic statistical models. With machine learning, we've made great progress in various fields, but this is not enough to realize true AI because we need to tell a machine what the features of objects to be classified are. The technique required for machine learning is called feature engineering. Then, deep learning came out, based on one machine learning algorithm - namely, neural networks. A machine can automatically learn what the features of objects are with deep learning, and thus deep learning is recognized as a very innovative technique. Studies of deep learning are becoming more and more active, and every day new technologies are invented. Some of the latest technologies are introduced in the last chapter of this book, *Chapter 8, What's Next?*, for reference.

Deep learning is often thought to be very complicated, but the truth is it's not. As mentioned, deep learning is the evolving technique of machine learning, and deep learning itself is very simple yet elegant. We'll look at more details of machine learning algorithms in the next chapter. With a great understanding of machine learning, you will easily acquire the essence of deep learning.

2
Algorithms for Machine Learning – Preparing for Deep Learning

In the previous chapter, you read through how deep learning has been developed by looking back through the history of AI. As you should have noticed, machine learning and deep learning are inseparable. Indeed, you learned that deep learning is the developed method of machine learning algorithms.

In this chapter, as a pre-exercise to understand deep learning well, you will see the mode details of machine learning, and in particular, you will learn the actual code for the method of machine learning, which is closely related to deep learning.

In this chapter, we will cover the following topics:

- The core concepts of machine learning
- An overview of popular machine learning algorithms, especially focusing on neural networks
- Theories and implementations of machine learning algorithms related to deep learning: perceptrons, logistic regression, and multi-layer perceptrons

Getting started

We will insert the source code of machine learning and deep learning with Java from this chapter. The version of JDK used in the code is 1.8, hence Java versions greater than 8 are required. Also, IntelliJ IDEA 14.1 is used for the IDE. We will use the external library from *Chapter 5, Exploring Java Deep Learning Libraries – DL4J, ND4J, and More*, so we are starting with a new Maven project.

The root package name of the code used in this book is DLWJ, the initials of *Deep Learning with Java*, and we will add a new package or a class under DLWJ as required. Please refer to the screenshot below, which shows the screen immediately after the new project is made:

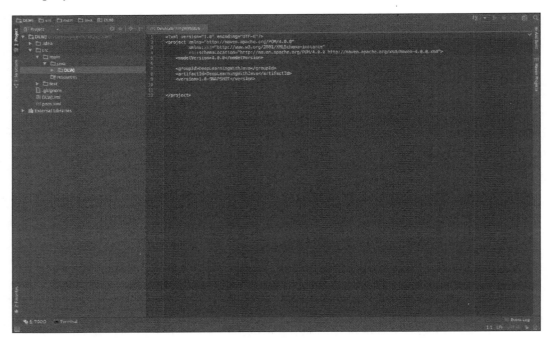

There will be some names of variables and methods in the code that don't follow the Java coding standard. This is to improve your understanding together with some characters in the formulas to increase readability. Please bear this in mind in advance.

The need for training in machine learning

You have already seen that machine learning is a method of pattern recognition. Machine learning reaches an answer by recognizing and sorting out patterns from the given learning data. It may seem easy when you just look at the sentence, but the fact is that it takes quite a long time for machine learning to sort out unknown data, in other words, to build the appropriate model. Why is that? Is it that difficult to just sort out? Does it even bother to have a "learning" phase in between?

The answer is, of course, yes. It is extremely difficult to sort out data appropriately. The more complicated a problem becomes, the more it becomes impossible to perfectly classify data. This is because there are almost infinite patterns of categorization when you simply say "pattern classifier." Let's look at a very simple example in the following graph:

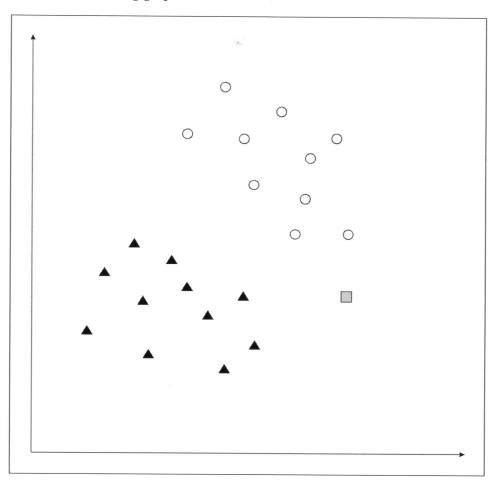

There are two types of data, circles and triangles, and the unknown data, the square. You don't know which group the square belongs to in the two-dimensional coordinate space, so the task is to find out which group the square belongs to.

You might instantly know that there seems to be a boundary that separates two data types. And if you decide where to set this boundary, it looks like you should be able to find out to which group the square belongs. Well then, let's decide the boundary. In reality, however, it is not so easy to clearly define this boundary. If you want to set a boundary, there are various lines to consider, as you can see in the following figure:

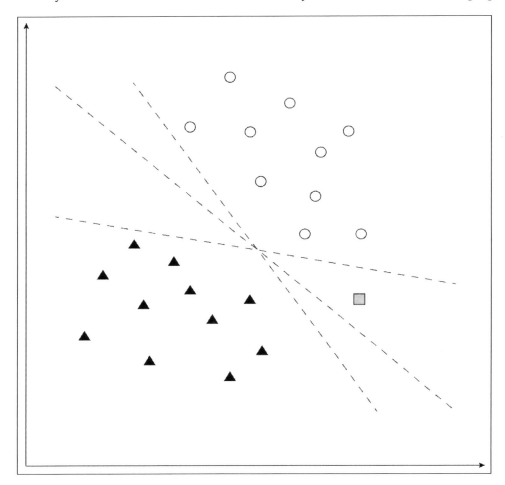

Additionally, depending on the placement of the boundary, you can see that the square might be allocated to a different group or pattern. Furthermore, it is also possible to consider that the boundary might be a nonlinear boundary.

In machine learning, what a machine does in training is choose the most likely boundary from these possible patterns. It will automatically learn how to sort out patterns when processing massive amounts of training data one after another. In other words, it adjusts the parameters of a mathematical model and eventually decides the boundary. The boundary decided by machine learning is called the **decision boundary** and is not necessarily a linear or nonlinear boundary. A decision boundary can also be a hyperplane if it classifies the data best. The more complicated the distribution of the data is, the more likely it is that the decision boundary would be nonlinear boundary or a hyperplane. A typical case is the multi-dimensional classification problem. We have already faced such difficulty by just setting a boundary in this simple problem, so it's not hard to imagine that it would be very time-consuming to solve a more complicated problem.

Supervised and unsupervised learning

In the previous section, we saw that there could be millions of boundaries even for a simple classification problem, but it is difficult to say which one of them is the most appropriate. This is because, even if we could properly sort out patterns in the known data, it doesn't mean that unknown data can also be classified in the same pattern. However, you can increase the percentage of correct pattern categorization. Each method of machine learning sets a standard to perform a better pattern classifier and decides the most possible boundary — the decision boundary — to increase the percentage. These standards are, of course, greatly varied in each method. In this section, we'll see what all the approaches we can take are.

First, machine learning can be broadly classified into **supervised learning** and **unsupervised learning**. The difference between these two categories is the dataset for machine learning is labeled data or unlabeled data. With supervised learning, a machine uses labeled data, the combination of input data and output data, and mentions which pattern each type of data is to be classified as. When a machine is given unknown data, it will derive what pattern can be applied and classify the data based on labeled data, that is, the past correct answers. As an example, in the field of image recognition, when you input some images into a machine, if you prepare and provide a certain number of images of a cat, labeled `cat`, and the same number of images of a human, labeled `human`, for a machine to learn, it can judge by itself which group out of cat or human (or none of them) that an image belongs to. Of course, just deciding whether the image is a cat or a human doesn't really provide a practical use, but if you apply the same approach to other fields, you can create a system that can automatically tag who is who in a photo uploaded on social media. As you can now see, in supervised training, the learning proceeds when a machine is provided with the correct data prepared by humans in advance.

On the other hand, with unsupervised learning, a machine uses unlabeled data. In this case, only input data is given. Then, what the machine learns is patterns and rules that the dataset includes and contains. The purpose of unsupervised learning is to grasp the structure of the data. It can include a process called **clustering**, which classifies a data constellation in each group that has a common character, or the process of extracting the correlation rule. For example, imagine there is data relating to a user's age, sex, and purchase trend for an online shopping website. Then, you might find out that the tastes of men in their 20s and women in their 40s are close, and you want to make use of this trend to improve your product marketing. We have a famous story here—it was discovered from unsupervised training that a large number of people buy beer and diapers at the same time.

You now know there are big differences between supervised learning and unsupervised learning, but that's not all. There are also different learning methods and algorithms for each learning method, respectively. Let's look at some representative examples in the following section.

Support Vector Machine (SVM)

You could say that SVM is the most popular supervised training method in machine learning. The method is still used for broad fields in the data mining industry. With SVM, data from each category located the closest to other categories is marked as the standard, and the decision boundary is determined using the standard so that the sum of the Euclidean distance from each marked data and the boundary is maximized. This marked data is called **support vectors**. Simply put, SVM sets the decision boundary in the middle point where the distance from every pattern is maximized. Therefore, what SVM does in its algorithm is known as **maximizing the margin**. The following is the figure of the concept of SVM:

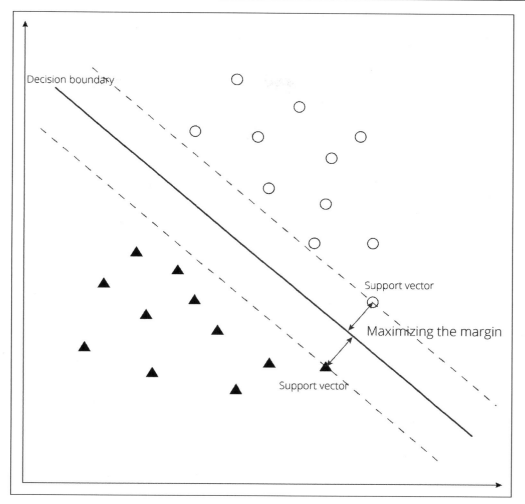

If you only hear this statement, you might think "is that it?" but what makes SVM the most valuable is a math technique: the kernel trick, or the kernel method. This technique takes the data that seems impossible to be classified linearly in the original dimension and intentionally maps it to a higher dimensional space so that it can be classified linearly without any difficulties. Take a look at the following figure so you can understand how the kernel trick works:

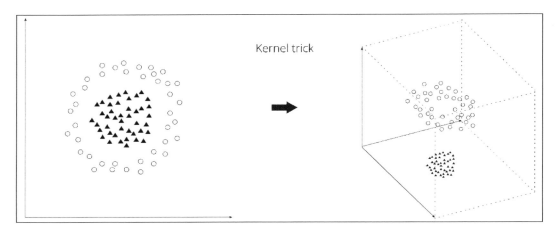

We have two types of data, represented by circles and triangles, and it is obvious that it would be impossible to separate both data types linearly in a two-dimensional space. However, as you can see in the preceding figure, by applying the kernel function to the data (strictly speaking, the feature vectors of training data), whole data is transformed into a higher dimensional space, that is, a three-dimensional space, and it is possible to separate them with a two-dimensional plane.

While SVM is useful and elegant, it has one demerit. Since it maps the data into a higher dimension, the number of calculations often increases, so it tends to take more time in processing as the calculation gets more complicated.

Hidden Markov Model (HMM)

HMM is an unsupervised training method that assumes data follows the **Markov process**. The Markov process is a stochastic process in which a future condition is decided solely on the present value and is not related to the past condition. HMM is used to predict which state the observation comes from when only one observation is visible.

The previous explanation alone may not help you fully understand how HMM works, so let's look at an example. HMM is often used to analyze a base sequence. You may know that a base sequence consists of four nucleotides, for example, A, T, G, C, and the sequence is actually a string of these nucleotides. You won't get anything just by looking through the string, but you do have to analyze which part is related to which gene. Let's say that if any base sequence is lined up randomly, then each of the four characters should be output by one-quarter when you cut out any part of the base sequence.

However, if there is a regularity, for example, where C tends to come next to G or the combination of ATT shows up frequently, then the probability of each character being output would vary accordingly. This regularity is the probability model and if the probability of being output relies only on an immediately preceding base, you can find out genetic information (= state) from a base sequence (= observation) using HMM.

Other than these bioinformatic fields, HMM is often used in fields where time sequence patterns, such as syntax analysis of **natural language processing** (**NLP**) or sound signal processing, are needed. We don't explore HMM deeper here because its algorithm is less related to deep learning, but you can reference a very famous book, *Foundations of statistical natural language processing*, from MIT Press if you are interested.

Neural networks

Neural networks are a little different to the machine learning algorithms. While other methods of machine learning take an approach based on probability or statistics, neural networks are algorithms that imitate the structure of a human brain. A human brain is made of a neuron network. Take a look at the following figure to get an idea of this:

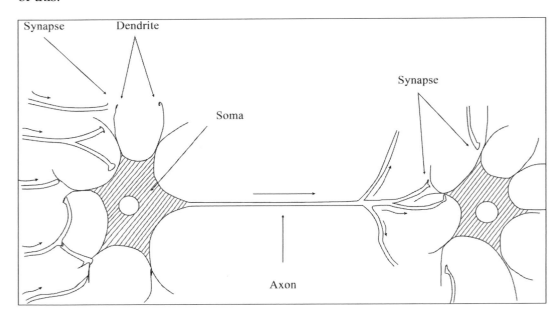

One neuron is linked to the network through another neuron and takes electrical stimulation from the synapse. When that electricity goes above the threshold, it gets ignited and transmits the electrical stimulation to the next neuron linked to the network. Neural networks distinguish things based on how electrical stimulations are transmitted.

Neural networks have originally been the type of supervised learning that represents this electrical stimulation with numbers. Recently, especially with deep learning, various types of neural networks algorithms have been introduced, and some of them are unsupervised learning. The algorithm increases the predictability by adjusting the weight of the networks through the process of learning. Deep learning is an algorithm based on neural networks. More details on neural networks will be explained later, with implementations.

Logistic regression

Logistic regression is one of the statistical regression models of variables with the Bernoulli distribution. While SVM and neural networks are classification models, logistic regression is a regression model, yet it certainly is one of the supervised learning methods. Although logistic regression has a different base of thinking, as a matter of fact, it can be thought of as one of the neural networks when you look at its formula. Details on logistic regression will also be explained with implementations later.

As you can see, each machine learning method has unique features. It's important to choose the right algorithm based on what you would like to know or what you would would like to use the data for. You can say the same of deep learning. Deep learning has different methods, so not only should you consider which the best method among them is, but you should also consider that there are some cases where you should not use deep learning. It's important to choose the best method for each case.

Reinforcement learning

Just for your reference, there is another method of machine learning called **reinforcement learning**. While some categorize reinforcement learning as unsupervised learning, others declare that all three learning algorithms, supervised learning, unsupervised learning, and reinforcement learning, should be divided into different types of algorithms, respectively. The following image shows the basic framework of reinforcement learning:

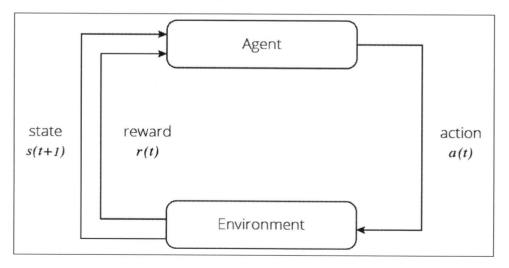

An agent takes an action based on the state of an environment and an environment will change based on the action. A mechanism with some sort of reward is provided to an agent following the change of an environment and the agent learns a better choice of act (decision-making).

Machine learning application flow

We have looked at the methods that machine learning has and how these methods recognize patterns. In this section, we'll see which flow is taken, or has to be taken, by data mining using machine learning. A decision boundary is set based on the model parameters in each of the machine learning methods, but we can't say that adjusting the model parameters is the only thing we have to care about. There is another troublesome problem, and it is actually the weakest point of machine learning: feature engineering. Deciding which features are to be created from raw data, that is, the analysis subject, is a necessary step in making an appropriate classifier. And doing this, which is the same as adjusting the model parameters, also requires a massive amount of trial and error. In some cases, feature engineering requires far more effort than deciding a parameter.

Thus, when we simply say "machine learning," there are certain tasks that need to be completed in advance as preprocessing to build an appropriate classifier to deal with actual problems. Generally speaking, these tasks can be summarized as follows:

- Deciding which machine learning method is suitable for a problem
- Deciding what features should be used
- Deciding which setting is used for model parameters

Only when these tasks are completed does machine learning become valuable as an application.

So, how do you decide the suitable features and parameters? How do you get a machine to learn? Let's first take a look at the following diagram as it might be easier for you to grasp the whole picture of machine learning. This is the summary of a learning flow:

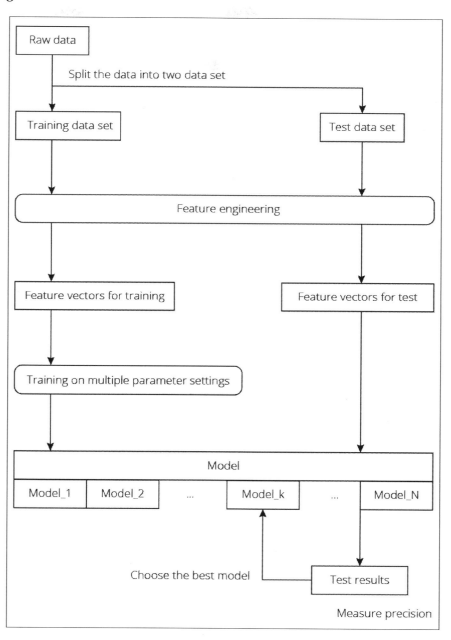

As you can see from the preceding image, the learning phase of machine learning can be roughly divided into these two steps:

- Training
- Testing

Literally, model parameters are renewed and adjusted in the training phase and the machine examines the merit of a model in the test phase. We have no doubt that the research or experiment will hardly ever succeed with just one training and one test set. We need to repeat the process of training → test, training → test ... until we get the right model.

Let's consider the preceding flowchart in order. First, you need to divide the raw data into two: a training dataset and a test dataset. What you need to be very careful of here is that the training data and the test data are separated. Let's take an example so you can easily imagine what this means: you are trying to predict the daily price of S&P 500 using machine learning with historical price data. (In fact, predicting the prices of financial instruments using machine learning is one of the most active research fields.)

Given that you have historical stock price data from 2001 to 2015 as raw data, what would happen if you performed the training with all the data from 2001 to 2015 and similarly performed the test for the same period? The situation would occur that even if you used simple machine learning or feature engineering, the probability of getting the right prediction would be 70%, or even higher at 80% or 90%. Then, you might think: *What a great discovery! The market is actually that simple! Now I can be a billionaire!*

But this would end as short-lived elation. The reality doesn't go that well. If you actually start investment management with that model, you wouldn't get the performance you were expecting and would be confused. This is obvious if you think about it and pay a little attention. If a training dataset and a test dataset are the same, you do the test with the data for which you already know the answer. Therefore, it is a natural consequence to get high precision, as you have predicted a correct answer using a correct answer. But this doesn't make any sense for a test. If you would like to evaluate the model properly, be sure to use data with different time periods, for example, you should use the data from 2001 to 2010 for the training dataset and 2011 to 2015 for the test. In this case, you perform the test using the data you don't know the answer for, so you can get a proper prediction precision rate. Now you can avoid going on your way to bankruptcy, believing in investments that will never go well.

So, it is obvious that you should separate a training dataset and a test dataset but you may not think this is a big problem. However, in the actual scenes of data mining, the case often occurs that we conduct an experiment with the same data without such awareness, so please be extra careful. We've talked about this in the case of machine learning, but it also applies to deep learning.

If you divide a whole dataset into two datasets, the first dataset to be used is the training dataset. To get a better precision rate, we first need to think about creating features in the training dataset. This feature engineering partly depends on human experience or intuition. It might take a long time and a lot of effort before you can choose the features to get the best results. Also, each machine learning method has different types of data formats of features to be accepted because the theory of models and formulas are unique to each method. As an example, we have a model that can only take an integer, a model that can only take a non-negative number/value, and a model that can only take real numbers from 0 to 1. Let's look back at the previous example of stock prices. Since the value of the price varies a lot within a broader range, it may be difficult to make a prediction with a model that can only take an integer.

Additionally, we have to be careful to ensure that there is compatibility between the data and the model. We don't say we can't use a model that can take all the real numbers from 0 if you would like to use a stock price as is for features. For example, if you divide all the stock price data by the maximum value during a certain period, the data range can fit into 0-1, hence you can use a model that can only take real numbers from 0 to 1. As such, there is a possibility that you can apply a model if you slightly change the data format. You need to keep this point in mind when you think about feature engineering. Once you create features and decide which method of machine learning to apply, then you just need to examine it.

In machine learning, features are, of course, important variables when deciding on the precision of a model; however, a model itself, in other words a formula within the algorithm, also has parameters. Adjusting the speed of learning or adjusting how many errors to be allowed are good examples of this. The faster the learning speed, the less time it takes to finish the calculation, hence it's better to be fast. However, making the learning speed faster means that it only provides solutions in brief. So, we should be careful not to lose our expected precision rates. Adjusting the permissible range of errors is effective for the case where a noise is blended in the data. The standard by which a machine judges "is this data weird?" is decided by humans.

Each method, of course, has a set of peculiar parameters. As for neural networks, how many neurons there should be in one of the parameters is a good example. Also, when we think of the kernel trick in SVM, how we set the kernel function is also one of the parameters to be determined. As you can see, there are so many parameters that machine learning needs to define, and which parameter is best cannot be found out in advance. In terms of how we define model parameters in advance, there is a research field that focuses on the study of parameters.

Therefore, we need to test many combinations of parameters to examine which combination can return the best precision. Since it takes a lot of time to test each combination one by one, the standard flow is to test multiple models with different parameter combinations in concurrent processing and then compare them. It is usually the case that a range of parameters that should be set to some extent is decided, so it's not that the problem can't be solved within a realistic time frame.

When the model that can get good precision is ready in the training dataset, next comes the test step. The rough flow of the test is to apply the same feature engineering applied to the training dataset and the same model parameters respectively and then verify the precision. There isn't a particularly difficult step in the test. The calculation doesn't take time either. It's because finding a pattern from data, in other words optimizing a parameter in a formula, creates a calculation cost. However, once a parameter adjustment is done, then the calculation is made right away as it only applies the formula to new datasets. The reason for performing a test is, simply put, to examine whether a model is too optimized by the training dataset. What does this mean? Well, in machine learning, there are two patterns where a training set goes well but a test set doesn't.

The first case is incorrect optimization by classifying noisy data blended into a training dataset. This can be related to the adjustment of a permissible range of errors mentioned earlier in this chapter. Data in the world is not usually clean. It can be said that there is almost no data that can be properly classified into clean patterns. The prediction of stock prices is a good example again. Stock prices usually repeat moderate fluctuations from previous stock prices, but sometimes they suddenly surge or drop sharply. And, there is, or should be, no regularity in this irregular movement. Another case is if you would like to predict the yield of a crop for a country; the data of the year affected by abnormal weather should be largely different from the normal years' data. These examples are extreme and easy to understand, but most for a data in the real world also contains noises, making it difficult to classify data into proper patterns. If you just do training without adjusting the parameters of machine learning, the model forces it to classify the noise data into a pattern. In this case, data from the training dataset might be classified correctly, but since noise data in the training dataset is also classified and the noise doesn't exist in the test dataset, the predictability in a test should be low.

The second case is incorrect optimizing by classifying data that is characteristic only in a training dataset. For example, let's think about making an app of English voice inputs. To build your app, you should prepare the data of pronunciation for various words as a training dataset. Now, let's assume you prepared enough voice data of British English native speakers and were able to create a high precision model that could correctly classify the pronunciation in the training dataset. The next step is a test. Since it's a test, let's use the voice data of American English native speakers for the means of providing different data. What would be the result then? You probably wouldn't get good precision. Furthermore, if you try the app to recognize the pronunciation of non-native speakers of English, the precision would be much lower. As you know, English has different pronunciations for different areas. If you don't take this into consideration and optimize the model with the training data set of British English, even though you may get a good result in the training set, you won't get a good result in the test set and it won't be useful for the actual application.

These two problems occur because the machine learning model learns from a training dataset and fits into the dataset too much. This problem is literally called the **overfitting problem**, and you should be very careful to avoid it. The difficulty of machine learning is that you have to think about how to avoid this overfitting problem besides the feature engineering. These two problems, overfitting and feature engineering, are partially related because poor feature engineering would fail into overfitting.

To avoid the problem of overfitting, there's not much to do except increase the amount of data or the number of tests. Generally, the amount of data is limited, so the methods of increasing the number of tests are often performed. The typical example is **K-fold cross-validation**. In K-fold cross-validation, all the data is divided into K sets at the beginning. Then, one of the datasets is picked as a test dataset and the rest, K-1, are put as training datasets. Cross-validation performs the verification on each dataset divided into K for K times, and the precision is measured by calculating the average of these K results. The most worrying thing is that both a training dataset and a test dataset may happen to have good precision by chance; however, the probability of this accident can be decreased in K-fold cross-validation as it performs a test several times. You can never worry too much about overfitting, so it's necessary that you verify results carefully.

Well, you have now read through the flow of training and test sets and learned key points to be kept in mind. These two mainly focus on data analysis. So, for example, if your purpose is to pull out the meaningful information from the data you have and make good use of it, then you can go through this flow. On the other hand, if you need an application that can cope with a further new model, you need an additional process to make predictions with a model parameter obtained in a training and a test set. As an example, if you would like to find out some information from a dataset of stock prices and analyze and write a market report, the next step would be to perform training and test sets. Or, if you would like to predict future stock prices based on the data and utilize it as an investment system, then your purpose would be to build an application using a model obtained in a training and a test set and to predict a price based on the data you can get anew every day, or from every period you set. In the second case, if you would like to renew the model with the data that is newly added, you need to be careful to complete the calculation of the model building by the time the next model arrives.

Theories and algorithms of neural networks

In the previous section, you saw the general flow of when we perform data analysis with machine learning. In this section, theories and algorithms of neural networks, one of the methods of machine learning, are introduced as a preparation toward deep learning.

Although we simply say "neural networks", their history is long. The first published algorithm of neural networks was called **perceptron**, and the paper released in 1957 by Frank Rosenblatt was named *The Perceptron: A Perceiving and Recognizing Automaton (Project Para)*. From then on, many methods were researched, developed, and released, and now neural networks are one of the elements of deep learning. Although we simply say "neural networks," there are various types and we'll look at the representative methods in order now.

Perceptrons (single-layer neural networks)

The perceptron algorithm is the model that has the simplest structure in the algorithms of neural networks and it can perform linear classification for two classes. We can say that it's the prototype of neural networks. It is the algorithm that models human neurons in the simplest way.

The following figure is a schematic drawing of the general model:

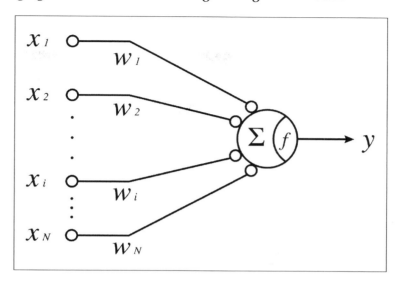

Here, x_i shows the input signal, w_i shows the weight corresponding to each input signal, and y shows the output signal. f is the activation function. Σ shows, literally, the meaning of calculating the sum of data coming from the input. Please bear in mind that x_i applies a processing of nonlinear conversion with feature engineering in advance, that is, x_i is an engineered feature.

Then, the output of perceptron can be represented as follows:

$$y(x) = f\left(w^T x\right)$$

$$f(a) = \begin{cases} +1, & a \geq 0 \\ -1, & a < 0 \end{cases}$$

$f(*)$ is called the step function. As shown in the equation, Perceptron returns the output by multiplying each factor of the feature vector by weight, calculating the sum of them, and then activating the sum with the step function. The output is the result estimated by Perceptron. During the training, you will compare this result with the correct data and feed back the error.

Let t be the value of the labeled data. Then, the formula can be represented as follows:

$$t \in \{-1, 1\}$$

If some labeled data belongs to class 1, C_1, we have $t = 1$. If it belongs to class 2, C_2, we have $t = -1$. Also, if the input data is classified correctly, we get:

$$\begin{cases} w^T x_n > 0 \ \ where \ x_n \in C_1 \\ w^T x_n < 0 \ \ where \ x_n \in C_2 \end{cases}$$

So, putting these equations together, we have the following equation of properly classified data:

$$w^T x_n t_n > 0$$

Therefore, you can increase the predictability of Perceptron by minimizing the following function:

$$E(w) = - \sum_{n \in M} w^T x_n t_n$$

Here, E is called the error function. M shows the set of misclassification. To minimize the error function, gradient descent, or steepest descent, an optimization algorithm is used to find a local minimum of a function using gradient descent. The equation can be described as follows:

$$w^{(k+1)} = w^{(k)} - n\nabla E(w) = w^{(k)} + \eta x_n t_n$$

Here, η is the learning rate, a common parameter of the optimization algorithm that adjusts the learning speed, and k shows the number of steps of the algorithm. In general, the smaller the value of the learning rate, the more probable it is that the algorithm falls into a local minimum because the model can't override the old value much. If the value is too big, however, the model parameters can't converge because the values fluctuate too widely. Therefore, practically, the learning rate is set to be big at the beginning and then dwindle with each iteration. On the other hand, with perceptrons, it is proved that the algorithm converges irrespective of the value of the learning rate when the data set is linearly separable, and thus the value is set to be 1.

Now, let's look at an implementation. The package structure is as follows:

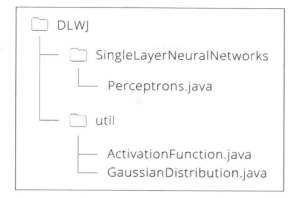

Let's have a look at the content of Perceptrons.java as shown in the previous image. We will look into the main methods one by one.

First, we define the parameters and constants that are needed for learning. As explained earlier, the learning rate (defined as learningRate in the code) can be 1:

```java
final int train_N = 1000;  // number of training data
final int test_N = 200;    // number of test data
final int nIn = 2;         // dimensions of input data

double[][] train_X = new double[train_N][nIn];  // input data for
training
int[] train_T = new int[train_N];                // output data (label)
for training

double[][] test_X = new double[test_N][nIn];  // input data for test
int[] test_T = new int[test_N];               // label of inputs
int[] predicted_T = new int[test_N];          // output data predicted
by the model

final int epochs = 2000;    // maximum training epochs
final double learningRate = 1.;  // learning rate can be 1 in
perceptrons
```

Needless to say, machine learning and deep learning need a dataset to be learned and classified. Here, since we would like to focus on implementations deeply related to the theory of perceptrons, a sample dataset is generated within the source code and is used for the training and test sets, the class called GaussianDistribution is defined, and it returns a value following the normal distribution or Gaussian distribution. As for the source code itself, we don't mention it here as you can see it in GaussianDistribution.java. We set the dimensions of the learning data in nIn = 2 and define two types of instances as follows:

```
GaussianDistribution g1 = new GaussianDistribution(-2.0, 1.0, rng);
GaussianDistribution g2 = new GaussianDistribution(2.0, 1.0, rng);
```

You can get the values that follow the normal distributions with a mean of -2.0 and a variance of 1.0 by g1.random() and a mean of 2.0 and a variance of 1.0 by g2.random().

With these values, 500 data attributes are generated in class 1 obtained by [g1.random(), g2.random()] and another 500 generated in class 2 obtained by [g2.random(), g1.random()]. Also, please bear in mind that each value of the class 1 label is 1 and of the class 2 label is -1. Almost all the data turns out to be a value around [-2.0, 2.0] for class 1 and [2.0, -2.0] for class 2; hence, they can be linearly separated, but some data can be blended near the other class as noise.

Now we have prepared the data, we can move on to building the model. The number of units in the input layer, nIn, is the argument used here to decide the model outline:

```
Perceptrons classifier = new Perceptrons(nIn);
```

Let's look at the actual Perceptrons constructor. The parameter of the perceptrons model is only the weight, w, of the network — very simple — as follows:

```
public Perceptrons(int nIn) {

    this.nIn = nIn;
    w = new double[nIn];

}
```

The next step is finally the training. The iteration of learning continues until it reaches enough numbers of the learning set in advance or classifies all the training data correctly:

```
while (true) {
    int classified_ = 0;

    for (int i=0; i < train_N; i++) {
```

```
        classified_ += classifier.train(train_X[i], train_T[i],
    learningRate);
        }

        if (classified_ == train_N) break;  // when all data classified
    correctly

        epoch++;
        if (epoch > epochs) break;
    }
```

In the `train` method, you can write down the gradient descent algorithm as we just explained. Here, the `w` parameter of the network is updated:

```
public int train(double[] x, int t, double learningRate) {

    int classified = 0;
    double c = 0.;

    // check whether the data is classified correctly
    for (int i = 0; i < nIn; i++) {
        c += w[i] * x[i] * t;
    }

    // apply gradient descent method if the data is wrongly classified
    if (c > 0) {
        classified = 1;
    } else {
        for (int i = 0; i < nIn; i++) {
            w[i] += learningRate * x[i] * t;
        }
    }

    return classified;
}
```

Once you have done enough numbers of learning and finish, the next step is to perform the test. First, let's check which class the test data is classified by in the well-trained model:

```
for (int i = 0; i < test_N; i++) {
    predicted_T[i] = classifier.predict(test_X[i]);
}
```

In the `predict` method, simply activate the input through the network. The step function used here is defined in `ActivationFunction.java`:

```java
public int predict (double[] x) {

    double preActivation = 0.;

    for (int i = 0; i < nIn; i++) {
        preActivation += w[i] * x[i];
    }

    return step(preActivation);
}
```

Subsequently, we evaluate the model using the test data. You might need more explanation to perform this part.

Generally, the performance of the method of machine learning is measured by the indicator of accuracy, precision, and recall based on the confusion matrix. The confusion matrix summarizes the results of a comparison of the predicted class and the correct class in the matrix and is shown as the following table:

	p_predicted	**n_predicted**
p_actual	True positive (TP)	False negative (FN)
n_actual	False positive (FP)	True negative (TN)

The three indicators are shown below:

$$Accuracy = \frac{TP + TN}{TP + TN + FP + FN}$$

$$Precision = \frac{TP}{TP + FP}$$

$$Recall = \frac{TP}{TP + FN}$$

Accuracy shows the proportion of the data that is correctly classified for all the data, while precision shows the proportion of the actual correct data to the data predicted as positive, and recall is the proportion of the data predicted as positive to the actual positive data. Here is the code for this:

```
int[][] confusionMatrix = new int[2][2];
double accuracy = 0.;
double precision = 0.;
double recall = 0.;

for (int i = 0; i < test_N; i++) {

    if (predicted_T[i] > 0) {
        if (test_T[i] > 0) {
            accuracy += 1;
            precision += 1;
            recall += 1;
            confusionMatrix[0][0] += 1;
        } else {
            confusionMatrix[1][0] += 1;
        }
    } else {
        if (test_T[i] > 0) {
            confusionMatrix[0][1] += 1;
        } else {
            accuracy += 1;
            confusionMatrix[1][1] += 1;
        }
    }

}

accuracy /= test_N;
precision /= confusionMatrix[0][0] + confusionMatrix[1][0];
recall /= confusionMatrix[0][0] + confusionMatrix[0][1];

System.out.println("---------------------------");
System.out.println("Perceptrons model evaluation");
System.out.println("---------------------------");
System.out.printf("Accuracy:  %.1f %%\n", accuracy * 100);
System.out.printf("Precision: %.1f %%\n", precision * 100);
System.out.printf("Recall:    %.1f %%\n", recall * 100);
```

When you compile `Perceptron.java` and run it, you can get 99.0% for accuracy, 98.0% for precision, and 100% for recall. This means that actual positive data is classified correctly but that there has been some data wrongly predicted as positive when it is actually negative. In this source code, since the data set is for demonstration, K-fold cross-validation is not included. The dataset in the example above is programmatically generated and has little noise data. Therefore, accuracy, precision, and recall are all high because the data can be well classified. However, as mentioned above, you have to look carefully at results, especially when you have great results.

Logistic regression

Logistic regression is, as you can assume from the name, the regression model. But when you look at the formula, you can see that logistic regression is the linear separation model that generalizes perceptrons.

Logistic regression can be regarded as one of the neural networks. With perceptrons, the step function is used for the activation function, but in logistic regression, the (logistic) sigmoid function is used. The equation of the sigmoid function can be represented as follows:

$$\sigma(x) = \frac{1}{1+e^{-x}}$$

The graph of this function can be illustrated as follows:

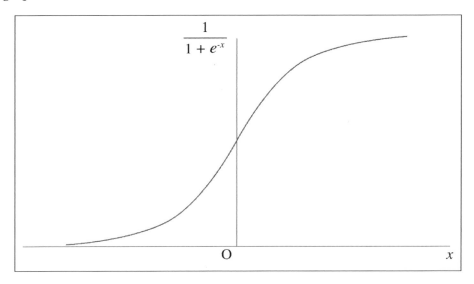

The `sigmoid` function maps any values of a real number to a value from 0 to 1. Therefore, the output of the logistic regression can be regarded as the posterior probability for each class. The equations can be described as follows:

$$p(C=1\,|\,x) = y(x) = \sigma\left(w^T x + b\right)$$

$$p(C=0\,|\,x) = 1 - p(C=1\,|\,x)$$

These equations can be combined to make:

$$p(C=t\,|\,x) = y^t\left(1-y\right)^{1-t}$$

Here, $t \in \{0,1\}$ is the correct data. You may have noticed that the range of the data is different from the one of perceptrons.

With the previous equation, the `likelihood` function, which estimates the maximum likelihood of the model parameters, can be expressed as follows:

$$L(w,b) = \prod_{n=1}^{N} y_n^{t_n}\left(1-y_n\right)^{1-t_n}$$

Where:

$$y_n = p(C=1\,|\,x_n)$$

As you can see, not only the weight of the network but the bias b are also parameters that need to be optimized.

What we need to do now is maximize the likelihood function, but the calculation is worrying because the function has a mathematical product. To make the calculation easier, we take the logarithm (log) of the likelihood function. Additionally, we substitute the sign to turn the object to minimizing the negative log `likelihood` function. Since the log is the monotonic increase, the magnitude correlation doesn't change. The equation can be represented as follows:

$$E\left(w,b\right) = -In\,L\left(w,b\right) = -\sum_{n=1}^{N}\left\{t_{n}In\,y_{n} + \left(1-t_{n}\right)In\left(1-y_{n}\right)\right\}$$

You can see the error function at the same time. This type of function is called a cross-entropy error function.

Similar to perceptrons, we can optimize the model by computing the gradients of the model parameters, w and b. The gradients can be described as follows:

$$\frac{\partial E\left(w,b\right)}{\partial w} = -\sum_{n=1}^{N}\left(t_{n} - y_{n}\right)x_{n}$$

$$\frac{\partial E\left(w,b\right)}{\partial b} = -\sum_{n=1}^{N}\left(t_{n} - y_{n}\right)$$

With these equations, we can update the model parameters as follows:

$$w^{(k+1)} = w^{(k)} - \eta\frac{\partial E\left(w,b\right)}{\partial w} = w^{(k)} + \eta\sum_{n=1}^{N}\left(t_{n} - y_{n}\right)x_{n}$$

$$b^{(k+1)} = b^{(k)} - \eta\frac{\partial E\left(w,b\right)}{\partial b} = b^{(k)} + \eta\sum_{n=1}^{N}\left(t_{n} - y_{n}\right)$$

Theoretically, we have no problem using the equations just mentioned and implementing them. As you can see, however, you have to calculate the sum of all the data to compute the gradients for each iteration. This will hugely increase the calculation cost once the size of a dataset becomes big.

Therefore, another method is usually applied that partially picks up some data from the dataset, computes the gradients by calculating the sum only with picked data, and renews the parameters. This is called **stochastic gradient descent** (SGD) because it stochastically chooses a subset of the data. This subset of the dataset used for one renewal is called a **mini-batch**.

SGD using a mini-batch is sometimes called **mini-batch stochastic gradient descent** (**MSGD**). Online training that learns to randomly choose one data from the dataset is called SGD to distinguish one from the other. In this book, however, both MSGD and SGD are called SGD, as both become the same when the size of the mini-batch is 1. Since learning by each data does increase the calculation cost, it's better to use mini-batches.

In terms of the implementation of logistic regression, since it can be covered with multi-class logistic regression introduced in the next section, we won't write the code here. You can refer to the code of multi-class logistic regression in this section.

Multi-class logistic regression

Logistic regression can also be applied to multi-class classification. In two-class classification, the activation function is the sigmoid function, and you can classify the data by evaluating the output value shifting from 0 to 1. How, then, can we classify data when the number of classes is K? Fortunately, it is not difficult. We can classify multi-class data by changing the equation for the output to the K-dimensional class-membership probability vector, and we use the `softmax` function to do so, which is the multivariate version of the sigmoid function. The posterior probability of each class can be represented as follows:

$$p\left(C = k \mid x\right) = y_k\left(x\right) = \frac{\exp\left(w_k^T x + b_k\right)}{\sum_{j=1}^{K} \exp\left(w_j^T x + b_j\right)}$$

With this, the same as two-class cases, you can get the likelihood function and the negative log likelihood function as follows:

$$L\left(W, b\right) = \prod_{n=1}^{N} \prod_{k=1}^{K} y_{nk}^{t_{nk}}$$

$$E(W,b) = -\ln L(W,b) = -\sum_{n=1}^{N}\sum_{k=1}^{K} t_{nk} \ln y_{nk}$$

Here, $W = \left[w_1, \ldots, w_j, \ldots, w_K \right]$, $y_{nk} = y_k(x_n)$. Also, t_{nk} is the Kth element of the correct data vector, t_n, which corresponds to the nth training data. If an input data belongs to the class k, the value of t_{nk} is 1; the value is 0 otherwise.

Gradients of the loss function against the model parameters, the weight vector, and the bias, can be described as follows:

$$\frac{\partial E}{\partial w_j} = -\sum_{n=1}^{N} \left(t_{nj} - y_{nj} \right) x_n$$

$$\frac{\partial E}{\partial b_j} = -\sum_{n=1}^{N} \left(t_{nj} - y_{nj} \right)$$

Now let's look through the source code to better understand the theory. You can see some variables related to mini-batches besides the ones necessary for the model:

```
int minibatchSize = 50;  //  number of data in each minibatch
int minibatch_N = train_N / minibatchSize; //  number of minibatches

double[][][] train_X_minibatch = new double[minibatch_N]
[minibatchSize][nIn];  // minibatches of training data
int[][][] train_T_minibatch = new int[minibatch_N][minibatchSize]
[nOut];         // minibatches of output data for training
```

The following code is the process to shuffle training data so the data of each mini-batch is to be applied randomly to SGD:

```
List<Integer> minibatchIndex = new ArrayList<>();  // data index for
minibatch to apply SGD
for (int i = 0; i < train_N; i++) minibatchIndex.add(i);
Collections.shuffle(minibatchIndex, rng);  // shuffle data index for
SGD
```

Since we can see the multi-class classification problem, we generate a sample dataset with three classes. In addition to mean values and variances used in perceptrons, we also use the dataset according to normal distribution with the mean of 0.0 and the variance of 1.0 for the training data and the test data for class 3. In other words, each class's data follows normal distributions with the mean of [-2.0, 2.0], [2.0, -1.0] and [0.0, 0.0] and the variance of 1.0. We defined the training data as the int type and the test data as the Integer type for the labeled data. This is to process the test data easier when evaluating the model. Also, each piece of labeled data is defined as an array because it follows multi-class classification:

```
train_T[i] = new int[]{1, 0, 0};
test_T[i] = new Integer[]{1, 0, 0};
```

Then we classify the training data into a mini-batch using minibatchIndex, which was defined earlier:

```
for (int i = 0; i < minibatch_N; i++) {
    for (int j = 0; j < minibatchSize; j++) {
        train_X_minibatch[i][j] = train_X[minibatchIndex.get(i *
minibatchSize + j)];
        train_T_minibatch[i][j] = train_T[minibatchIndex.get(i *
minibatchSize + j)];
    }
}
```

Now we have prepared the data, let's practically build a model:

```
LogisticRegression classifier = new LogisticRegression(nIn, nOut);
```

The model parameters of logistic regression are W, weight of the network, and bias b:

```
public LogisticRegression(int nIn, int nOut) {

    this.nIn = nIn;
    this.nOut = nOut;

    W = new double[nOut][nIn];
    b = new double[nOut];

}
```

The training is done with each mini-batch. If you set minibatchSize = 1, you can make the training so-called online training:

```
for (int epoch = 0; epoch < epochs; epoch++) {
    for (int batch = 0; batch < minibatch_N; batch++) {
```

```
        classifier.train(train_X_minibatch[batch], train_T_
minibatch[batch], minibatchSize, learningRate);
    }
    learningRate *= 0.95;
}
```

Here, the learning rate gradually decreases so that the model can converge. Now, for the actual training `train` method, you can briefly divide it into two parts, as follows:

1. Calculate the gradient of `W` and `b` using the data from the mini-batch.

2. Update `W` and `b` with the gradients:

```
// 1. calculate gradient of W, b
for (int n = 0; n < minibatchSize; n++) {

    double[] predicted_Y_ = output(X[n]);

    for (int j = 0; j < nOut; j++) {
        dY[n][j] = predicted_Y_[j] - T[n][j];

        for (int i = 0; i < nIn; i++) {
            grad_W[j][i] += dY[n][j] * X[n][i];
        }

        grad_b[j] += dY[n][j];
    }
}

// 2. update params
for (int j = 0; j < nOut; j++) {
    for (int i = 0; i < nIn; i++) {
        W[j][i] -= learningRate * grad_W[j][i] / minibatchSize;
    }
    b[j] -= learningRate * grad_b[j] / minibatchSize;
}

return dY;
```

At the end of the `train` method, `return dY`, the error value of the predicted data and the correct data is returned. This is not mandatory for logistic regression itself but it is necessary in the machine learning and the deep learning algorithms introduced later.

Next up for the training is the test. The process of performing the test doesn't really change from the one for perceptrons.

First, with the `predict` method, let's predict the input data using the trained model:

```
for (int i = 0; i < test_N; i++) {
   predicted_T[i] = classifier.predict(test_X[i]);
}
```

The `predict` method and the `output` method called are written as follows:

```
public Integer[] predict(double[] x) {

    double[] y = output(x);  // activate input data through learned
networks
    Integer[] t = new Integer[nOut]; // output is the probability, so
cast it to label

    int argmax = -1;
    double max = 0.;

    for (int i = 0; i < nOut; i++) {
        if (max < y[i]) {
            max = y[i];
            argmax = i;
        }
    }

    for (int i = 0; i < nOut; i++) {
        if (i == argmax) {
            t[i] = 1;
        } else {
            t[i] = 0;
        }
    }

    return t;
}


public double[] output(double[] x) {

    double[] preActivation = new double[nOut];

    for (int j = 0; j < nOut; j++) {

        for (int i = 0; i < nIn; i++) {
            preActivation[j] += W[j][i] * x[i];
```

```
        }

        preActivation[j] += b[j];   // linear output
    }

    return softmax(preActivation, nOut);
}
```

First, input data is activated with the output method. As you can see from the bottom of the output, the activation function uses the softmax function. softmax is defined in ActivationFunction.java, and with this function the array showing the probability of each class is returned, hence you just need to get the index within the array of the element that has the highest probability. The index represents the predicted class.

Finally, let's evaluate the model. Again, the confusion matrix is introduced for model evaluation, but be careful as you need to find the precision or recall for each class this time because we have multi-class classification here:

```
int[][] confusionMatrix = new int[patterns][patterns];
double accuracy = 0.;
double[] precision = new double[patterns];
double[] recall = new double[patterns];

for (int i = 0; i < test_N; i++) {
    int predicted_ = Arrays.asList(predicted_T[i]).indexOf(1);
    int actual_ = Arrays.asList(test_T[i]).indexOf(1);

    confusionMatrix[actual_][predicted_] += 1;
}

for (int i = 0; i < patterns; i++) {
    double col_ = 0.;
    double row_ = 0.;

    for (int j = 0; j < patterns; j++) {

        if (i == j) {
            accuracy += confusionMatrix[i][j];
            precision[i] += confusionMatrix[j][i];
            recall[i] += confusionMatrix[i][j];
        }

        col_ += confusionMatrix[j][i];
        row_ += confusionMatrix[i][j];
```

```
    }
    precision[i] /= col_;
    recall[i] /= row_;
}

accuracy /= test_N;

System.out.println("----------------------------------");
System.out.println("Logistic Regression model evaluation");
System.out.println("----------------------------------");
System.out.printf("Accuracy: %.1f %%\n", accuracy * 100);
System.out.println("Precision:");
for (int i = 0; i < patterns; i++) {
    System.out.printf(" class %d: %.1f %%\n", i+1, precision[i] * 100);
}
System.out.println("Recall:");
for (int i = 0; i < patterns; i++) {
    System.out.printf(" class %d: %.1f %%\n", i+1, recall[i] * 100);
```

Multi-layer perceptrons (multi-layer neural networks)

Single-layer neural networks have a huge problem. Perceptrons or logistic regressions are efficient for problems that can be linearly classified but they can't solve nonlinear problems at all. For example, they can't even solve the simplest XOR problem seen in the figure here:

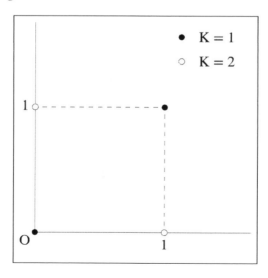

Since most of the problems in the real world are nonlinear, perceptrons and logistic regression aren't applicable for practical uses. Hence, the algorithm was improved to correspond to nonlinear problems. These are multi-layer perceptrons (or **multi-layer neural networks, MLPs**). As you can see from the name, by adding another layer, called a hidden layer, between the input layer and the output layer, the networks have the ability to express various patterns. This is the graphical model of an MLP:

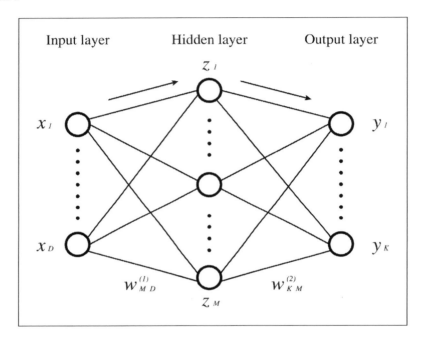

What is most important here is not to introduce the skip-layer connection. In neural networks, it is better for both theory and implementation to keep the model as having a feed-forward network structure. By sticking to these rules, and by increasing the number of hidden layers, you can approximate arbitrary functions without making the model too complicated mathematically.

Now, let's see how we compute the output. It looks complicated at first glance but it accumulates the layers and the scheme of the network's weight or activation in the same way, so you simply have to combine the equation of each layer. Each output can be shown as follows:

$$E\left(W,b\right) = -In\,L\left(W,b\right) = -\sum_{n=1}^{N}\sum_{k=1}^{K}t_{nk}\,In\,Y_{nk}$$

Here, h is the activation function of the hidden layer and g is the output layer.

As has already been introduced, in the case of multi-class classification, the activation function of the output layer can be calculated efficiently by using the `softmax` function, and the error function is given as follows:

$$y_k = g\left(\sum_{j=1}^{M} w_{kj}^{(2)} z_j + b_k^{(2)}\right)$$
$$= g\left(\sum_{j=1}^{M} w_{kj}^{(2)} h\left(\sum_{i=1}^{D} w_{ji}^{(1)} x_i + b_j^{(1)}\right) + b_k^{(2)}\right)$$

As for a single layer, it's fine just to reflect this error in the input layer, but for the multi-layer, neural networks cannot learn as a whole unless you reflect the error in both the hidden layer and input layer.

Fortunately, in feed-forward networks, there is an algorithm known as `backpropagation`, which enables the model to propagate this error efficiently by tracing the network forward and backward. Let's look at the mechanism of this algorithm. To make the equation more readable, we'll think about the valuation of an error function in the online training, shown as follows:

$$E\left(W,b\right) = \sum_{n=1}^{N} E_n\left(W,b\right)$$

We can now think about just the gradient of this, E_n. Since all the data in a dataset in most cases of practical application is independent and identically distributed, we have no problem defining it as we just mentioned.

Each unit in the feed-forward network is shown as the sum of the weight of the network connected to the unit, hence the generalized term can be represented as follows:

$$a_j = \sum_i w_{ji} x_i + b_j$$

$$z_j = h\left(a_j\right)$$

Be careful, as x_i here is not only the value of the input layer (of course, this can be the value of the input layer). Also, h is the nonlinear activation function. The gradient of weights and the gradient of the bias can be shown as follows:

$$\frac{\partial E_n}{\partial w_{ji}} = \frac{\partial E_n}{\partial a_j} \frac{\partial a_j}{\partial w_{ji}} = \frac{\partial E_n}{\partial a_j} x_i$$

$$\frac{\partial E_n}{\partial b_j} = \frac{\partial E_n}{\partial a_j} \frac{\partial a_j}{\partial b_j} = \frac{\partial E_n}{\partial a_j}$$

Now, let the notation defined in the next equation be introduced:

$$\delta_j := \frac{\partial E_n}{\partial a_j}$$

Then, we get:

$$\frac{\partial E_n}{\partial w_{ji}} = \delta_j x_i$$

$$\frac{\partial E_n}{\partial b_j} = \delta_j$$

Therefore, when we compare the equations, the output unit can be described as follows:

$$\delta_k = y_k - t_k$$

Also, each unit of the hidden layer is:

$$\delta_j = \frac{\partial E_n}{\partial a_j} = \sum_k \frac{\partial E_n}{\partial a_k} \frac{\partial a_k}{\partial a_j}$$

$$\delta_j = h'(a_j) \sum_k w_{kj} \delta_k$$

Thus, the **backpropagation formula** is introduced. As such, delta is called the **backpropagated** error. By computing the `backpropagated` error, the weights and bias can be calculated. It may seem difficult when you look at the formula, but what it basically does is receive feedback on errors from a connected unit and renew the weight, so it's not that difficult.

Now, let's look at an implementation with a simple XOR problem as an example. You will have better understanding when you read the source code. The structure of the package is as follows:

```
📁 DLWJ
        📁 MultiLayerNeuralNetworks
            ── MultiLayerPerceptrons.java
            ── HiddenLayer.java

        📁 SingleLayerNeuralNetworks
            ── LogisticRegression.java

    📁 util
            ── ActivationFunction.java
            ── RandomGenerator.java
```

The basic flow of the algorithm is written in `MultiLayerPerceptrons.java`, but the actual part of backpropagation is written in `HiddenLayer.java`. We use multi-class logistic regression for the output layer. Since there is no change in `LogisticRegression.java`, the code is not shown in this section. In `ActivationFunction.java`, derivatives of the sigmoid function and hyperbolic tangent are added. The hyperbolic tangent is also the activation function that is often used as an alternative to the sigmoid. Also, in `RandomGenerator.java`, the method to generate random numbers with a uniform distribution is written. This is to randomly initialize the weight of the hidden layer, and it is quite an important part because a model often falls into a local optimum and fails to classify the data depending on these initial values.

Let's have a look at the content of `MultiLayerPerceptrons.java`. In `MultiLayerPereptrons.java`, differently defined classes are defined respectively for each layer: `HiddenLayer` class is used for the hidden layer and `LogisticRegression` class for the output layer. Instances of these classes are defined as `hiddenLayer` and `logisticLayer`, respectively:

```
public MultiLayerPerceptrons(int nIn, int nHidden, int nOut, Random
rng) {

    this.nIn = nIn;
    this.nHidden = nHidden;
    this.nOut = nOut;

    if (rng == null) rng = new Random(1234);
    this.rng = rng;

    // construct hidden layer with tanh as activation function
    hiddenLayer = new HiddenLayer(nIn, nHidden, null, null, rng,
"tanh");  // sigmoid or tanh

    // construct output layer i.e. multi-class logistic layer
    logisticLayer = new LogisticRegression(nHidden, nOut);

}
```

The parameters of the MLP are the weights W and bias b of the hidden layer, HiddenLayer, and the output layer, LogisticRegression. Since the output layer is the same as the one previously introduced, we won't look at the code here. The constructor of HiddenLayer is as follows:

```
public HiddenLayer(int nIn, int nOut, double[][] W, double[] b, Random
rng, String activation) {

    if (rng == null) rng = new Random(1234);  // seed random

    if (W == null) {

        W = new double[nOut][nIn];
        double w_ = 1. / nIn;

        for(int j = 0; j < nOut; j++) {
            for(int i = 0; i < nIn; i++) {
                W[j][i] = uniform(-w_, w_, rng);  // initialize W with
uniform distribution
            }
        }

    }

    if (b == null) b = new double[nOut];

    this.nIn = nIn;
    this.nOut = nOut;
    this.W = W;
    this.b = b;
    this.rng = rng;

    if (activation == "sigmoid" || activation == null) {

        this.activation = (double x) -> sigmoid(x);
        this.dactivation = (double x) -> dsigmoid(x);

    } else if (activation == "tanh") {

        this.activation = (double x) -> tanh(x);
        this.dactivation = (double x) -> dtanh(x);

    } else {
```

```
        throw new IllegalArgumentException("activation function not
    supported");
        }


    }
```

W is initialized, randomly matching the number of the units. This initialization is actually tricky as it makes you face the local minima problem more often if the initial values are not well distributed. Therefore, in a practical scene, it often happens that the model is tested with some random seeds. The activation function can be applied to either the sigmoid function or the hyperbolic tangent function.

The training of the MLP can be given by forward propagation and backward propagation through the neural networks in order:

```
public void train(double[][] X, int T[][], int minibatchSize, double
learningRate) {

    double[][] Z = new double[minibatchSize][nIn];  // outputs of
hidden layer (= inputs of output layer)
    double[][] dY;

    // forward hidden layer
    for (int n = 0; n < minibatchSize; n++) {
        Z[n] = hiddenLayer.forward(X[n]);  // activate input units
    }

    // forward & backward output layer
    dY = logisticLayer.train(Z, T, minibatchSize, learningRate);

    // backward hidden layer (backpropagate)
    hiddenLayer.backward(X, Z, dY, logisticLayer.W, minibatchSize,
learningRate);
}
```

The part of `hiddenLayer.backward` gives the hidden layer backpropagation of the prediction error, dY, from a logistic regression. Be careful, as the input data of a logistic regression is also necessary for the backpropagation:

```
public double[][] backward(double[][] X, double[][] Z, double[][] dY,
double[][] Wprev, int minibatchSize, double learningRate) {

    double[][] dZ = new double[minibatchSize][nOut];  //
backpropagation error

    double[][] grad_W = new double[nOut][nIn];
```

```
double[] grad_b = new double[nOut];

// train with SGD
// calculate backpropagation error to get gradient of W, b
for (int n = 0; n < minibatchSize; n++) {

    for (int j = 0; j < nOut; j++) {

        for (int k = 0; k < dY[0].length; k++) {   // k < ( nOut of
previous layer )
            dZ[n][j] += Wprev[k][j] * dY[n][k];
        }
        dZ[n][j] *= dactivation.apply(Z[n][j]);


        for (int i = 0; i < nIn; i++) {
            grad_W[j][i] += dZ[n][j] * X[n][i];
        }

        grad_b[j] += dZ[n][j];
    }
}

// update params
for (int j = 0; j < nOut; j++) {
    for(int i = 0; i < nIn; i++) {
        W[j][i] -= learningRate * grad_W[j][i] / minibatchSize;
    }
    b[j] -= learningRate * grad_b[j] / minibatchSize;
}

return dZ;
}
```

You might think the algorithm is complex and difficult because the arguments seem complicated, but what we do here is almost the same as what we do with the `train` method of logistic regression: we calculate the gradients of `W` and `b` with the unit of the mini-batch and update the model parameters. That's it. So, can an MLP learn the XOR problem? Check the result by running `MultiLayerPerceptrons.java`.

The result only outputs the percentages of the accuracy, precision, and recall of the model, but for example, if you dump the prediction data with the `predict` method of `LogisticRegression`, you can see how much it actually predicts the probability, as follows:

```
double[] y = output(x);   // activate input data through learned
networks
Integer[] t = new Integer[nOut]; // output is the probability, so cast
it to label

System.out.println(  Arrays.toString(y) );
```

We've just shown that MLPs can approximate the function of XOR. Moreover, it is proven that MLPs can approximate any functions. We don't follow the math details here, but you can easily imagine that the more units MLPs have, the more complicated functions they could express and approximate.

Summary

In this chapter, as preparation for deep learning, we dug into neural networks, which are one of the algorithms of machine learning. You learned about three representative algorithms of single-layer neural networks: perceptrons, logistic regression, and multi-class logistic regression. We see that single-layer neural networks can't solve nonlinear problems, but this problem can be solved with multi-layer neural networks — the networks with a hidden layer(s) between the input layer and output layer. An intuitive understanding of why MLPs can solve nonlinear problems says that the networks can learn more complicated logical operations by adding layers and increasing the number of units, and thus having the ability to express more complicated functions. The key to letting the model have this ability is the backpropagation algorithm. By backpropagating the error of the output to the whole network, the model is updated and adjusted to fit in the training data with each iteration, and finally optimized to approximate the function for the data.

In the next chapter, you'll learn the concepts and algorithms of deep learning. Since you've now acquired a foundational understanding of machine learning algorithms, you'll have no difficulty learning about deep learning.

3
Deep Belief Nets and Stacked Denoising Autoencoders

From this chapter through to the next chapter, you are going to learn the algorithms of deep learning. We'll follow the fundamental math theories step by step to fully understand each algorithm. Once you acquire the fundamental concepts and theories of deep learning, you can easily apply them to practical applications.

In this chapter, the topics you will learn about are:

- Reasons why deep learning could be a breakthrough
- The differences between deep learning and past machine learning (neural networks)
- Theories and implementations of the typical algorithms of deep learning, **deep belief nets** (DBN), and **Stacked Denoising Autoencoders (SDA)**

Neural networks fall

In the previous chapter, you learned about the typical algorithm of neural networks and saw that nonlinear classification problems cannot be solved with perceptrons but can be solved by making multi-layer modeled neural networks. In other words, nonlinear problems can be learned and solved by inserting a hidden layer between the input and output layer. There is nothing else to it; but by increasing the number of neurons in a layer, the neural networks can express more patterns as a whole. If we ignore the time cost or an over-fitting problem, theoretically, neural networks can approximate any function.

So, can we think this way? If we increase the number of hidden layers—accumulate hidden layers over and over—can neural networks solve any complicated problem? It's quite natural to come up with this idea. And, as a matter of course, this idea has already been examined. However, as it turns out, this trial didn't work well. Just accumulating layers didn't make neural networks solve the world's problems. On the contrary, some cases have less accuracy when predicting than others with fewer layers.

Why do these cases happen? It's not wrong for neural networks with more layers to have more expression. So, where is the problem? Well, it is caused because of the feature that learning algorithms have in feed-forward networks. As we saw in the previous chapter, the backpropagation algorithm is used to propagate the learning error into the whole network efficiently with the multi-layer neural networks. In this algorithm, an error is reversed in each layer of the neural network and is conveyed to the input layer one by one in order. By backpropagating the error at the output layer to the input layer, the weight of the network is adjusted at each layer in order and the whole weight of a network is optimized.

This is where the problem occurs. If the number of layers of a network is small, an error backpropagating from an output layer can contribute to adjusting the weights of each layer well. However, once the number of layers increases, an error gradually disappears every time it backpropagates layers, and doesn't adjust the weight of the network. At a layer near the input layer, an error is not fed back at all.

The neural networks where the link among layers is dense have an inability to adjust weights. Hence, the weight of the whole of the networks cannot be optimized and, as a matter of course, the learning cannot go well. This serious problem is known as the **vanishing gradient problem** and has troubled researchers as a huge problem that the neural network had for a long time until deep learning showed up. The neural network algorithm reached a limit at an early stage.

Neural networks' revenge

Because of the vanishing gradient problem, neural networks lost their popularity in the field of machine learning. We can say that the number of cases used for data mining in the real world by neural networks was remarkably small compared to other typical algorithms such as logistic regression and SVM.

But then deep learning showed up and broke all the existing conventions. As you know, deep learning is the neural network accumulating layers. In other words, it is deep neural networks, and it generates astounding predictability in certain fields. Now, speaking of AI research, it's no exaggeration to say that it's the research into deep neural networks. Surely it's the counterattack by neural networks. If so, why didn't the vanishing gradient problem matter in deep learning? What's the difference between this and the past algorithm?

In this section, we'll look at why deep learning can generate such predictability and its mechanisms.

Deep learning's evolution – what was the breakthrough?

We can say that there are two algorithms that triggered deep learning's popularity. The first one, as mentioned in *Chapter 1, Deep Learning Overview*, is DBN pioneered by Professor Hinton (https://www.cs.toronto.edu/~hinton/absps/fastnc.pdf). The second one is SDA, proposed by Vincent et al. (http://www.iro.umontreal.ca/~vincentp/Publications/denoising_autoencoders_tr1316.pdf). SDA was introduced a little after the introduction of DBN. It also recorded high predictability even with deep layers by taking a similar approach to DBN, although the details of the algorithm are different.

So, what is the common approach that solved the vanishing gradient problem? Perhaps you are nervously preparing to solve difficult equations in order to understand DBN or SDA, but don't worry. DBN is definitely an algorithm that is understandable. On the contrary, the mechanism itself is really simple. Deep learning was established by a very simple and elegant solution. The solution is: **layer-wise training**. That's it. You might think it's obvious if you see it, but this is the approach that made deep learning popular.

As mentioned earlier, in theory if there are more units or layers of neural networks, it should have more expressions and increase the number of problems it is able to solve. It doesn't work well because an error cannot be fed back to each layer correctly and parameters, as a whole network, cannot be adjusted properly. This is where the innovation was brought in for learning at a respective layer. Because each layer adjusts the weights of the networks independently, the whole network (that is, the parameters of the model) can be optimized properly even though the numbers of layers are piled up.

Previous models didn't go well because they tried to backpropagate errors from an output layer to an input layer straight away and tried to optimize themselves by adjusting the weights of the network with backpropagated errors. So, the algorithm shifted to layer-wise training and then the model optimization went well. That's what the breakthrough was for deep learning.

However, although we simply say **layer-wise training**, we need techniques for how to implement the learning. Also, as a matter of course, parameter adjustments for whole networks can't only be done with layer-wise training. We need the final adjustment. This phase of layer-wise training is called **pre-training** and the last adjustment phase is called **fine-tuning**. We can say that the bigger feature introduced in DBN and SDA is pre-training, but these two features are both part of the the necessary flow of deep learning. How do we do pre-training? What can be done in fine-tuning? Let's take a look at these questions one by one.

Deep learning with pre-training

Deep learning is more like neural networks with accumulated hidden layers. The layer-wise training in pre-training undertakes learning at each layer. However, you might still have the following questions: if both layers are hidden (that is, neither of the layers are input nor output layers), then how is the training done? What can the input and output be?

Before thinking of these questions, remind yourself of the following point again (reiterated persistently): deep learning is neural networks with piled up layers. This mean, model parameters are still the weights of the network (and bias) in deep learning. Since these weights (and bias) need to be adjusted among each layer, in the standard three layered neural network (that is, the input layer, the hidden layer, and the output layer), we need to optimize only the weights between the input layer and the hidden layer and between the hidden layer and the output layer. In deep learning, however, the weight between two hidden layers also needs to be adjusted.

First of all, let's think about the input of a layer. You can imagine this easily with a quick thought. The value propagated from the previous layer will become the input as it is. The value propagated from the previous layer is none other than the value forward propagated from the previous layers to the current layer by using the weight of the network, the same as in general feed-forward networks. It looks simple in writing, but you can see that it has an important meaning if you step into it further and try to understand what it means. The value from the previous layer becomes the input, which means that the features the previous layer(s) learned become the input of the current layer, and from there the current layer newly learns the feature of the given data. In other words, in deep learning, features are learned from the input data in stages (and semi-automatically). This implies a mechanism where the deeper a layer becomes, the higher the feature it learns. This is what normal multi-layer neural networks couldn't do and the reason why it is said "a machine can learn a concept."

Now, let's think about the output. Please bear in mind that thinking about the output means thinking about how it learns. DBN and SDA have completely different approaches to learning, but both fill the following condition: to learn in order to equate output values and input values. You might think "What are you talking about?" but this is the technique that makes deep learning possible.

The value comes and goes back to the input layer through the hidden layer, and the technique is to adjust the weight of the networks (that is, to equate the output value and the input value) to eliminate the error at that time. The graphical model can be illustrated as follows:

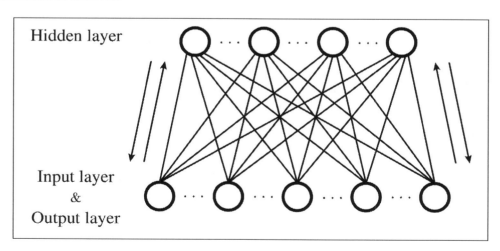

It looks different from standard neural networks at a glance, but there's nothing special. If we intentionally draw the diagram of the input layer and the output layer separately, the mechanism is the same shape as the normal neural network:

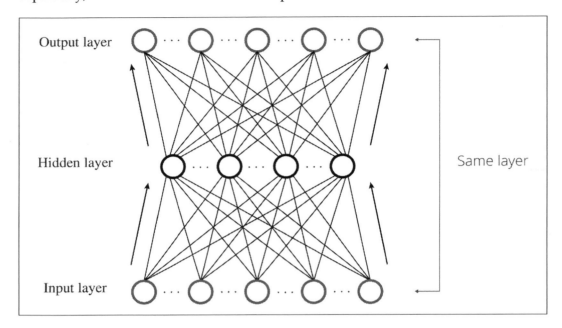

For a human, this action of *matching input and output* is not intuitive, but for a machine it is a valid action. If so, how it can learn features from input data by matching the output layer and input layer?

Need a little explanation? Let's think about it this way: in the algorithm of machine learning, including neural networks, learning intends to minimize errors between the model's prediction output and the dataset output. The mechanism is to remove an error by finding a pattern from the input data and making data with a common pattern the same output value (for example, 0 or 1). What would then happen if we turned the output value into the input value?

When we look at problems that should be solved as a whole through deep learning, input data is, fundamentally, a dataset that can be divided into some patterns. This means that there are some common features in the input data. If so, in the process of learning where each output value becomes respective input data, the weight of networks should be adjusted to focus more on the part that reflects the common features. And, even within the data categorized in the same class, learning should be processed to reduce weight on the non-common feature part, that is, the noise part.

Now you should understand what the input and output is in a certain layer and how learning progresses. Once the pre-training is done at a certain layer, the network moves on to learning in the next layer. However, as you can see in the following images, please also keep in mind that a hidden layer becomes an input layer when the network moves to learning in the next layer:

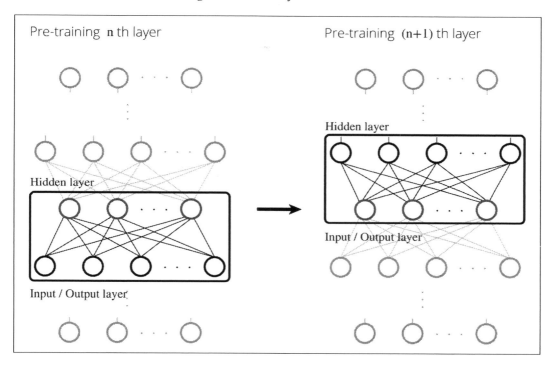

The point here is that the layer after the pre-training can be treated as normal feed-forward neural networks where the weight of the networks is adjusted. Hence, if we think about the input value, we can simply calculate the value forward propagated from the input layer to the current layer through the network.

Up to now, we've looked through the flow of pre-training (that is, layer-wise training). In the hidden layers of deep neural networks, features of input data are extracted in stages through learning where the input matches the output. Now, some of you might be wondering: I understand that features can be learned in stages from input data by pre-training, but that alone doesn't solve the classification problem. So, how can it solve the classification problem?

Well, during pre-training, the information pertaining to which data belongs to which class is not provided. This means the pre-training is unsupervised training and it just analyzes the hidden pattern using only input data. This is meaningless if it can't be used to solve the problem however it extracts features. Therefore, the model needs to complete one more step to solve classification problems properly. That is fine-tuning. The main roles of fine-tuning are the following:

1. To add an output layer to deep neural networks that completed pre-training and to perform supervised training.

2. To do final adjustments for the whole deep neural network.

This can be illustrated as follows:

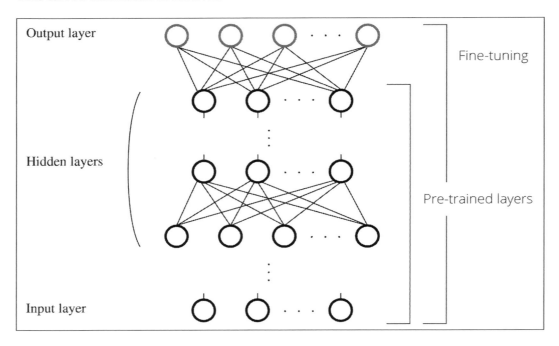

The supervised training in an output layer uses a machine learning algorithm, such as logistic regression or SVM. Generally, logistic regression is used more often considering the balance of the amount of calculation and the precision gained.

In fine-tuning, sometimes only the weights of an output layer will be adjusted, but normally the weights of whole neural networks, including the layer where the weights have been adjusted in pre-training, will also be adjusted. This means the standard learning algorithm, or in other words the backpropagation algorithm, is applied to the deep neural networks just as one multi-layer neural network. Thus, the model of neural networks with the problem of solving more complicated classification is completed.

Even so, you might have the following questions: why does learning go well with the standard backpropagation algorithm even in multi-layer neural networks where layers are piled up? Doesn't the vanishing gradient problem occur? These questions can be solved by pre-training. Let's think about the following: in the first place, the problem is that the weights of each network are not correctly adjusted due to improperly fed back errors in multi-layer neural networks without pre-training; in other words, the multi-layer neural networks where the vanishing gradient problem occurs. On the other hand, once the pre-training is done, the learning starts from the point where the weight of the network is almost already adjusted. Therefore, a proper error can be propagated to a layer close to an input layer. Hence the name fine-tuning. Thus, through pre-training and fine-tuning, eventually deep neural networks become neural networks with increased expression by having deep layers.

From the next section onwards, we will finally look through the theory and implementation of DBN and SDA, the algorithms of deep learning. But before that, let's look back at the flow of deep learning once again. Below is the summarized diagram of the flow:

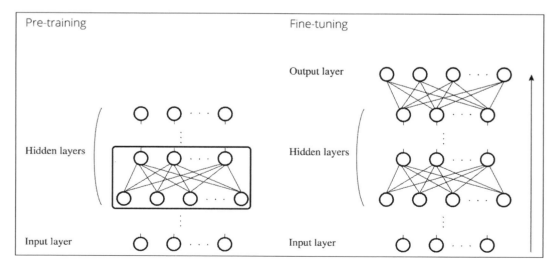

The parameters of the model are optimized layer by layer during pre-training and then adjusted as single deep neural networks during fine-tuning. Deep learning, the breakthrough of AI, is a very simple algorithm.

Deep learning algorithms

Now, let's look through the theory and implementation of deep learning algorithms. In this chapter, we will see DBN and SDA (and the related methods). These algorithms were both researched explosively, mainly between 2012 and 2013 when deep learning started to spread out rapidly and set the trend of deep learning on fire. Even though there are two methods, the basic flow is the same and consistent with pre-training and fine-tuning, as explained in the previous section. The difference between these two is which pre-training (that is, unsupervised training) algorithm is applied to them.

Therefore, if there could be difficult points in deep learning, it should be the theory and equation of the unsupervised training. However, you don't have to be afraid. All the theories and implementations will be explained one by one, so please read through the following sections carefully.

Restricted Boltzmann machines

The method used in the layer-wise training of DBN, pre-training, is called **Restricted Boltzmann Machines (RBM)**. To begin with, let's take a look at the RBM that forms the basis of DBN. As RBM stands for Restricted Boltzmann Machines, of course there's a method called **Boltzmann Machines (BMs)**. Or rather, BMs are a more standard form and RBM is the special case of them. Both are one of the neural networks and both were proposed by Professor Hinton.

The implementation of RBM and DBNs can be done without understanding the detailed theory of BMs, but in order to understand these concepts, we'll briefly look at the idea BMs are based on. First of all, let's look at the following figure, which shows a graphical model of BMs:

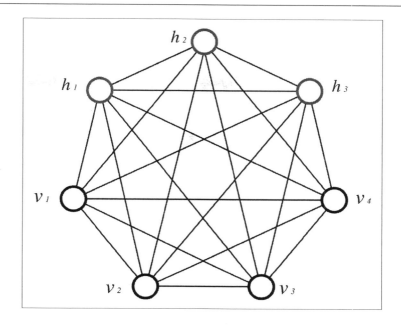

BMs look intricate because they are fully connected, but they are actually just simple neural networks with two layers. By rearranging all the units in the networks to get a better understanding, BMs can be shown as follows:

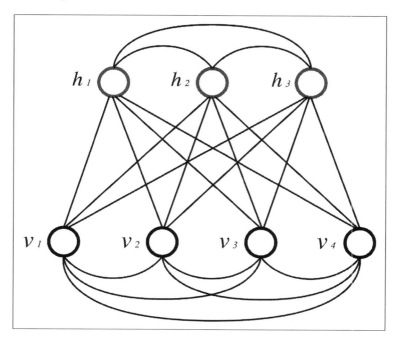

Please bear in mind that normally the input/output layer is called the **visible layer** in BMs and RBMs (a hidden layer is commonly used as it is), for it is the networks that presume the hidden condition (unobservable condition) from the observable condition. Also, the neurons of the visible layer are called **visible units** and the neurons of the hidden layer are called **hidden units**. Signs in the previous figure are described to match the given names.

As you can see in the diagram, the structure of BMs is not that different from standard neural networks. However, its way of thinking has a big feature. The feature is to adopt the concept of *energy* in neural networks. Each unit has a stochastic state respectively and the whole of the networks' energy is determined depending on what state each unit takes. (The first model that adopted the concept of energy in networks is called the **Hopfield network**, and BMs are the developed version of it. Since details of the Hopfield network are not totally relevant to deep learning, it is not explained in this book.) The condition that memorizes the correct data is the steady state of networks and the least amount of energy these networks have. On the other hand, if data with noise is provided to the network, each unit has a different state, but not a steady state, hence its condition makes the transition to stabilize the whole network, in other words, to transform it into a steady state.

This means that the weights of the model are adjusted and the state of each unit is transferred to minimize the energy function the networks have. These operations can remove the noise and extract the feature from inputs as a whole. Although the energy of networks sounds enormous, it's not too difficult to imagine because minimizing the energy function has the same effect as minimizing the error function.

The concept of BMs was wonderful, but various problems occurred when BMs were actually applied to practical problems. The biggest problem was that BMs are fully connected networks and take an enormous amount of calculation time. Therefore, RBM was devised. RBM is the algorithm that can solve various problems in a realistic time frame by making BMs restricted. Just as in BM, RBM is a model based on the energy of a network. Let's look at RBM in the diagram below:

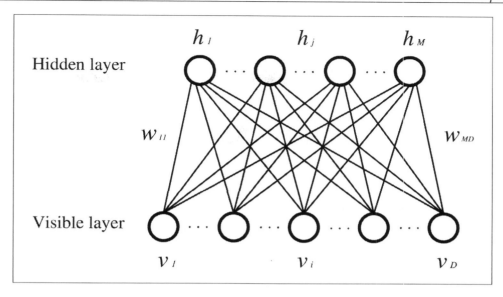

Here, D is the number of units in the visible layer and M the number of units in the hidden layer. v_i denotes the value of a visible unit, h_j the value of a hidden unit, and w_{ji} the weight between these two units. As you can see, the difference between BM and RBM is that RBM doesn't have connections between the same layer. Because of this restriction, the amount of calculation decreases and it can be applied to realistic problems.

Now, let's look through the theory.

> Be careful that, as a prerequisite, the value that each visible
> unit and hidden unit in RBM can take is generally {0, 1}, that is,
> binary (this is the same as BMs).

If we expand the theory, it can also handle continuous values. However, this could make equations complex, where it's not the core of the theory and where it's implemented with binary in the original DBN proposed by Professor Hinton. Therefore, we'll also implement binary RBM in this book. RBM with binary inputs is sometimes called **Bernoulli RBM**.

RBM is the energy-based model, and the status of a visible layer or hidden layer is treated as a stochastic variable. We'll look at the equations in order. First of all, each visible unit is propagated to the hidden units throughout a network. At this time, each hidden unit takes a binary value based on the probability distribution generated in accordance with its propagated inputs:

$$p\left(h_j = 1 \mid v\right) = \sigma\left(\sum_{i=1}^{D} w_{ij} v_i + c_j\right)$$

Here, c_j is the bias in a hidden layer and σ denotes the sigmoid function.

This time, it was conversely propagated from a hidden layer to a visible layer through the same network. As in the previous case, each visible unit takes a binary value based on probability distribution generated in accordance with propagated values.

$$p\left(v_i = 1 \mid h\right) = \sigma\left(\sum_{j=1}^{M} w_{ij} h_j + b_i\right)$$

Here, b_i is the bias of the visible layer. This value of visible units is expected to match the original input values. This means if W, the weight of the network as a model parameter, and b, c, the bias of a visible layer and a hidden layer, are shown as a vector parameter, θ, it leans θ in order for the probability $p\left(v \mid \theta\right)$ that can be obtained above to get close to the distribution of v.

For this learning, the energy function, that is, the evaluation function, needs to be defined. The energy function is shown as follows:

$$E\left(v, h\right) = -b^T v - c^T h - h^T W v$$

$$= -\sum_{i=1}^{D} b_i v_i - \sum_{j=1}^{M} c_j h_j - \sum_{j=1}^{M} \sum_{i=1}^{D} h_j w_{ij} v_i$$

Also, the joint probability density function showing the demeanor of a network can be shown as follows:

$$p(v,h) = \frac{1}{Z}\exp\big(-E(v,h)\big)$$

$$Z = \sum_{v,h}\exp\big(-E(v,h)\big)$$

From the preceding formulas, the equations for the training of parameters will be determined. We can get the following equation:

$$p(v\,|\,\theta) = \sum_{h}P(v,h) = \frac{1}{Z} = \sum_{h}\exp\big(-E(v,h)\big)$$

Hence, the **log likelihood** can be shown as follows:

$$In\,L(\theta\,|\,v) = In\,p(v\,|\,\theta)$$

$$= In\frac{1}{Z}\sum_{h}\exp\big(-E(v,h)\big)$$

$$= In\frac{1}{Z}\sum_{h}\exp\big(-E(v,h)\big) - In\sum_{v,h}\exp\big(-E(v,h)\big)$$

Then, we'll calculate each gradient against the model parameter. The derivative can be calculated as follows:

$$\frac{\partial In\, L(\theta\,|\,v)}{\partial \theta} = \frac{\partial}{\partial \theta}\left(In\sum_h \exp\left(-E(v,h)\right)\right) - \frac{\partial}{\partial \theta}\left(In\sum_{v,h}\exp\left(-E(v,h)\right)\right)$$

$$= -\frac{1}{\sum_h \exp\left(-E(v,h)\right)}\sum_h \exp\left(-E(v,h)\right)\frac{\partial E(v,h)}{\partial \theta}$$

$$= +\frac{1}{\sum_h \exp\left(-E(v,h)\right)}\sum_{v,h}\exp\left(-E(v,h)\right)\frac{\partial E(v,h)}{\partial \theta}$$

$$= -\sum_h p(h\,|\,v)\frac{\partial E(v,h)}{\partial \theta} + \sum_{v,h} p(v\,|\,h)\frac{\partial E(v,h)}{\partial \theta}$$

Some equations in the middle are complicated, but it turns out to be simple with the term of the probability distribution of the model and the original data.

Therefore, the gradient of each parameter is shown as follows:

$$\frac{\partial In\, L(\theta\,|\,v)}{\partial w_{ij}} = \sum_h p(h\,|\,v)\frac{\partial E(v,h)}{\partial w_{ij}} + \sum_{v,h} p(h\,|\,v)\frac{\partial E(v,h)}{\partial w_{ij}}$$

$$= \sum_h p(h\,|\,v)h_j v_i - \sum_v p(v)\sum_h p(h\,|\,v)h_j v_i$$

$$= p\left(H_j = 1\,|\,v\right)v_i - \sum_v p(v)p\left(H_j = 1\,|\,v\right)v_i$$

$$\frac{\partial In\, L(\theta\,|\,v)}{\partial b_i} = v_i - \sum_v p(v)v_i$$

$$\frac{\partial In\, L(\theta\,|\,v)}{\partial c_j} = p\left(H_j = 1\,|\,v\right) - \sum_v p(v)p\left(H_j = 1\,|\,v\right)$$

Now then, we could find the equation of the gradient, but a problem occurs when we try to apply this equation as it is. Think about the term of $\sum_v p(v)$. This term implies that we have to calculate the probability distribution for all the {0, 1} patterns, which can be assumed as input data that includes patterns that don't actually exist in the data.

We can easily imagine how this term can cause a combinatorial explosion, meaning we can't solve it within a realistic time frame. To solve this problem, the method for approximating data using Gibbs sampling, called **Contrastive Divergence (CD)**, was introduced. Let's look at this method now.

Here, $v^{(0)}$ is an input vector. Also, $v^{(k)}$ is an input (output) vector that can be obtained by sampling for k-times using this input vector.

Then, we get:

$$h_j^{(k)} \sim p\left(h_j \mid v^{(k)}\right)$$

$$h_i^{(k+1)} \sim p\left(v_i \mid h^{(k)}\right)$$

Hence, when approximating $p(v)$ after reiterating Gibbs sampling, the derivative of the log likelihood function can be represented as follows:

$$\frac{\partial \ln L(\theta \mid v)}{\partial \theta} = -\sum_h p(h \mid v)\frac{\partial E(v,h)}{\partial \theta} + \sum_{v,h} p(v,h)\frac{\partial E(v,h)}{\partial \theta}$$

$$\approx -\sum_h p\left(h \mid v^{(0)}\right)\frac{\partial E(v,h)}{\partial \theta}\sum_{v,h} p\left(h, v^{(k)}\right)\frac{\partial E\left(v^{(k)},h\right)}{\partial \theta}$$

Therefore, the model parameter can be shown as follows:

$$w_{ij}^{(\tau+1)} = w_{ij}^{(\tau)} + \eta \left(p\left(H_j = 1 \,|\, v^{(0)}\right) v_i^{(0)} - p\left(H_j = 1 \,|\, v^k\right) v_i^k \right)$$

$$b_i^{(\tau+1)} = b_i^{(\tau)} + \eta \left(v_i^{(0)} - v_i^k \right)$$

$$c_j^{(\tau+1)} = c_j^{(\tau)} + \eta \left(p\left(H_j = 1 \,|\, v^{(0)}\right) - p\left(H_j = 1 \,|\, v^k\right) \right)$$

Here, τ is the number of iterations and η is the learning rate. As shown in the preceding formulas, generally, CD that performs sampling k-times is shown as CD-k. It's known that CD-1 is sufficient when applying the algorithm to realistic problems.

Now, let's go through the implementation of RMB. The package structure is as shown in the following screenshot:

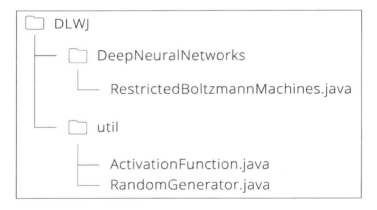

Let's look through the RestrictedBoltzmannMachines.java file. Because the first part of the main method just defines the variables needed for a model and generates demo data, we won't look at it here.

So, in the part where we generate an instance of a model, you may notice there are many null values in arguments:

```
// construct RBM
RestrictedBoltzmannMachines nn = new
RestrictedBoltzmannMachines(nVisible, nHidden, null, null, null,
rng);
```

When you look at the constructor, you might know that these `null` values are the RBM's weight matrix, bias of hidden units, and bias of visible units. We define arguments as `null` here because they are for DBN's implementation. In the constructor, these are initialized as follows:

```
if (W == null) {

    W = new double[nHidden][nVisible];
    double w_ = 1. / nVisible;

    for (int j = 0; j < nHidden; j++) {
        for (int i = 0; i < nVisible; i++) {
            W[j][i] = uniform(-w_, w_, rng);
        }
    }
}

if (hbias == null) {
    hbias = new double[nHidden];

    for (int j = 0; j < nHidden; j++) {
        hbias[j] = 0.;
    }
}

if (vbias == null) {
    vbias = new double[nVisible];

    for (int i = 0; i < nVisible; i++) {
        vbias[i] = 0.;
    }
}
```

The next step is training. CD-1 is applied for each mini-batch:

```
// train with contrastive divergence
for (int epoch = 0; epoch < epochs; epoch++) {
    for (int batch = 0; batch < minibatch_N; batch++) {
        nn.contrastiveDivergence(train_X_minibatch[batch],
minibatchSize, learningRate, 1);
    }
    learningRate *= 0.995;
}
```

Now, let's look into the essential point of RBM, the `contrastiveDivergence` method. CD-1 can obtain a sufficient solution when we actually run this program (and so we have k = 1 in the demo), but this method is defined to deal with CD-k as well:

```
// CD-k : CD-1 is enough for sampling (i.e. k = 1)
sampleHgivenV(X[n], phMean_, phSample_);

for (int step = 0; step < k; step++) {

    // Gibbs sampling
    if (step == 0) {
        gibbsHVH(phSample_, nvMeans_, nvSamples_, nhMeans_,
nhSamples_);
    } else {
        gibbsHVH(nhSamples_, nvMeans_, nvSamples_, nhMeans_,
nhSamples_);
    }

}
```

It appears that two different types of method, `sampleHgivenV` and `gibbsHVH`, are used in CD-k, but when you look into `gibbsHVH`, you can see:

```
public void gibbsHVH(int[] h0Sample, double[] nvMeans, int[]
nvSamples, double[] nhMeans, int[] nhSamples) {
    sampleVgivenH(h0Sample, nvMeans, nvSamples);
    sampleHgivenV(nvSamples, nhMeans, nhSamples);
}
```

So, CD-k consists of only two methods for sampling, `sampleVgivenH` and `sampleHgivenV`.

As the name of the method indicates, `sampleHgivenV` is the method that sets the probability distribution and sampling data generated in a hidden layer based on the given value of visible units and vice versa:

```
public void sampleHgivenV(int[] v0Sample, double[] mean, int[] sample)
{

    for (int j = 0; j < nHidden; j++) {
        mean[j] = propup(v0Sample, W[j], hbias[j]);
        sample[j] = binomial(1, mean[j], rng);
    }

}
```

```
public void sampleVgivenH(int[] h0Sample, double[] mean, int[] sample)
{

    for(int i = 0; i < nVisible; i++) {
        mean[i] = propdown(h0Sample, i, vbias[i]);
        sample[i] = binomial(1, mean[i], rng);
    }
}
```

The `propup` and `propdown` tags that set values to respective means are the method that activates values of each unit by the `sigmoid` function:

```
public double propup(int[] v, double[] w, double bias) {

    double preActivation = 0.;

    for (int i = 0; i < nVisible; i++) {
        preActivation += w[i] * v[i];
    }
    preActivation += bias;

    return sigmoid(preActivation);
}

public double propdown(int[] h, int i, double bias) {

    double preActivation = 0.;

    for (int j = 0; j < nHidden; j++) {
        preActivation += W[j][i] * h[j];
    }
    preActivation += bias;

    return sigmoid(preActivation);
}
```

The `binomial` method that sets a value to a sample is defined in `RandomGenerator. java`. The method returns 0 or 1 based on the binomial distribution. With this method, a value of each unit becomes binary:

```
public static int binomial(int n, double p, Random rng) {
    if(p < 0 || p > 1) return 0;

    int c = 0;
```

```
        double r;

        for(int i=0; i<n; i++) {
            r = rng.nextDouble();
            if (r < p) c++;
        }

        return c;
    }
```

Once approximated values are obtained by sampling, what we need to do is just calculate the gradient of a `model` parameter and renew a parameter using a mini-batch. There's nothing special here:

```
// calculate gradients
for (int j = 0; j < nHidden; j++) {
    for (int i = 0; i < nVisible; i++) {
        grad_W[j][i] += phMean_[j] * X[n][i] - nhMeans_[j] * nvSamples_
[i];
    }

    grad_hbias[j] += phMean_[j] - nhMeans_[j];
}

for (int i = 0; i < nVisible; i++) {
    grad_vbias[i] += X[n][i] - nvSamples_[i];
}


// update params
for (int j = 0; j < nHidden; j++) {
    for (int i = 0; i < nVisible; i++) {
        W[j][i] += learningRate * grad_W[j][i] / minibatchSize;
    }

    hbias[j] += learningRate * grad_hbias[j] / minibatchSize;
}

for (int i = 0; i < nVisible; i++) {
    vbias[i] += learningRate * grad_vbias[i] / minibatchSize;
}
```

Now we're done with the `model` training. Next comes the test and evaluation in general cases, but note that the model cannot be evaluated with barometers such as accuracy because RBM is a generative model. Instead, let's briefly look at how noisy data is changed by RBM here. Since RBM after training can be seen as a neural network, the weights of which are adjusted, the model can obtain reconstructed data by simply propagating input data (that is, noisy data) through a network:

```java
public double[] reconstruct(int[] v) {

    double[] x = new double[nVisible];
    double[] h = new double[nHidden];

    for (int j = 0; j < nHidden; j++) {
        h[j] = propup(v, W[j], hbias[j]);
    }

    for (int i = 0; i < nVisible; i++) {
        double preActivation_ = 0.;

        for (int j = 0; j < nHidden; j++) {
            preActivation_ += W[j][i] * h[j];
        }
        preActivation_ += vbias[i];

        x[i] = sigmoid(preActivation_);
    }

    return x;
}
```

Deep Belief Nets (DBNs)

DBNs are deep neural networks where logistic regression is added to RBMS as the output layer. Since the theory necessary for implementation has already been explained, we can go directly to the implementation. The package structure is as follows:

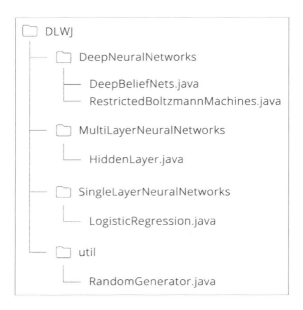

The flow of the program is very simple. The order is as follows:

1. Setting up parameters for the model.
2. Building the model.
3. Pre-training the model.
4. Fine-tuning the model.
5. Testing and evaluating the model.

Just as in RBM, the first step in setting up the main method is the declaration of variables and the code for creating demo data (the explanation is omitted here).

Please check that in the demo data, the number of units for an input layer is 60, a hidden layer has 2 layers, their combined number of units is 20, and the number of units for an output layer is 3. Now, let's look through the code from the *Building the Model* section:

```
// construct DBN
System.out.print("Building the model...");
DeepBeliefNets classifier = new DeepBeliefNets(nIn, hiddenLayerSizes,
nOut, rng);
Sy

stem.out.println("done.");
```

The variable of `hiddenLayerSizes` is an array and its length represents the number of hidden layers in deep neural networks. The deep learning algorithm takes a huge amount of calculation, hence the program gives us an output of the current status so that we can see which process is proceeding. The variable of `hiddenLayerSizes` is an array and its length represents the number of hidden layers in deep neural networks. Each layer is constructed in the constructor.

 Please bear in mind that `sigmoidLayers` and `rbmLayers` are, of course, different objects but their weights and bias are shared.

This is because, as explained in the theory section, pre-training performs layer-wise training, whereas the whole model can be regarded as one neural network:

```
// construct multi-layer
for (int i = 0; i < nLayers; i++) {
    int nIn_;
    if (i == 0) nIn_ = nIn;
    else nIn_ = hiddenLayerSizes[i-1];

    // construct hidden layers with sigmoid function
    //    weight matrices and bias vectors will be shared with RBM
layers
    sigmoidLayers[i] = new HiddenLayer(nIn_, hiddenLayerSizes[i], null,
null, rng, "sigmoid");

    // construct RBM layers
```

```
        rbmLayers[i] = new RestrictedBoltzmannMachines(nIn_,
hiddenLayerSizes[i], sigmoidLayers[i].W, sigmoidLayers[i].b, null,
rng);
    }

    // logistic regression layer for output
    logisticLayer = new LogisticRegression(hiddenLayerSizes[nLayers-1],
nOut);
```

The first thing to do after building the model is pre-training:

```
    // pre-training the model
    System.out.print("Pre-training the model...");
    classifier.pretrain(train_X_minibatch, minibatchSize, train_
minibatch_N, pretrainEpochs, pretrainLearningRate, k);
    System.out.println("done.");
```

Pre-training needs to be processed with each minibatch but, at the same time, with each layer. Therefore, all training data is given to the pretrain method first, and then the data of each mini-batch is processed in the method:

```
public void pretrain(int[][][] X, int minibatchSize, int minibatch_N,
int epochs, double learningRate, int k) {

    for (int layer = 0; layer < nLayers; layer++) {  // pre-train
layer-wise
        for (int epoch = 0; epoch < epochs; epoch++) {
            for (int batch = 0; batch < minibatch_N; batch++) {

                int[][] X_ = new int[minibatchSize][nIn];
                int[][] prevLayerX_;

                // Set input data for current layer
                if (layer == 0) {
                    X_ = X[batch];
                } else {

                    prevLayerX_ = X_;
                    X_ = new int[minibatchSize]
[hiddenLayerSizes[layer-1]];

                    for (int i = 0; i < minibatchSize; i++) {
                        X_[i] = sigmoidLayers[layer-1].
outputBinomial(prevLayerX_[i], rng);
```

```
            }
        }

            rbmLayers[layer].contrastiveDivergence(X_,
minibatchSize, learningRate, k);
          }
        }
    }

  }
```

Since the actual learning is done through CD-1 of RBM, the description of DBN within the code is very simple. In DBN (RBM), units of each layer have binary values, so the output method of `HiddenLayer` cannot be used because it returns double. Hence, the `outputBinomial` method is added to the class, which returns the `int` type (the code is omitted here). Once the pre-training is complete, the next step is fine-tuning.

 Be careful not to use training data that was used in the pre-training.

We can easily fall into overfitting if we use the whole data set for both pre-training and fine-tuning. Therefore, the validation data set is prepared separately from the training dataset and is used for fine-tuning:

```
// fine-tuning the model
System.out.print("Fine-tuning the model...");
for (int epoch = 0; epoch < finetuneEpochs; epoch++) {
    for (int batch = 0; batch < validation_minibatch_N; batch++) {
        classifier.finetune(validation_X_minibatch[batch],
        validation_T_minibatch[batch], minibatchSize,
        finetuneLearningRate);
    }
    finetuneLearningRate *= 0.98;
}
System.out.println("done.");
```

In the `finetune` method, the backpropagation algorithm in multi-layer neural networks is applied where the logistic regression is used for the output layer. To backpropagate unit values among multiple hidden layers, we define variables to maintain each layer's inputs:

```java
public void finetune(double[][] X, int[][] T, int minibatchSize,
double learningRate) {

    List<double[][]> layerInputs = new ArrayList<>(nLayers + 1);
    layerInputs.add(X);

    double[][] Z = new double[0][0];
    double[][] dY;

    // forward hidden layers
    for (int layer = 0; layer < nLayers; layer++) {

        double[] x_;  // layer input
        double[][] Z_ = new
        double[minibatchSize][hiddenLayerSizes[layer]];

        for (int n = 0; n < minibatchSize; n++) {

            if (layer == 0) {
                x_ = X[n];
            } else {
                x_ = Z[n];
            }

            Z_[n] = sigmoidLayers[layer].forward(x_);
        }

        Z = Z_.clone();
        layerInputs.add(Z.clone());
    }

    // forward & backward output layer
    dY = logisticLayer.train(Z, T, minibatchSize, learningRate);

    // backward hidden layers
    double[][] Wprev;
```

```
        double[][] dZ = new double[0][0];

    for (int layer = nLayers - 1; layer >= 0; layer--) {

        if (layer == nLayers - 1) {
            Wprev = logisticLayer.W;
        } else {
            Wprev = sigmoidLayers[layer+1].W;
            dY = dZ.clone();
        }

        dZ = sigmoidLayers[layer].backward(layerInputs.get(layer),
        layerInputs.get(layer+1), dY, Wprev, minibatchSize,
        learningRate);
    }
}
```

The training part of DBN is just how it is seen in the preceding code. The hard part is probably the theory and implementation of RBM, so you might think it's not too hard when you just look at the code of DBN.

Since DBN after the training can be regarded as one (deep) neural network, you simply need to forward propagate data in each layer when you try to predict which class the unknown data belongs to:

```
public Integer[] predict(double[] x) {

    double[] z = new double[0];

    for (int layer = 0; layer < nLayers; layer++) {

        double[] x_;

        if (layer == 0) {
            x_ = x;
        } else {
            x_ = z.clone();
        }

        z = sigmoidLayers[layer].forward(x_);
    }

    return logisticLayer.predict(z);
}
```

As for evaluation, no explanation should be needed because it's not much different from the previous classifier model.

Congratulations! You have now acquired knowledge of one of the deep learning algorithms. You might be able to understand it more easily than expected. However, the difficult part of deep learning is actually setting up the parameters, such as setting how many hidden layers there are, how many units there are in each hidden layer, the learning rate, the iteration numbers, and so on. There are way more parameters to set than in the method of machine learning. Please remember that you might find this point difficult when you apply this to a realistic problem.

Denoising Autoencoders

The method used in pre-training for SDA is called **Denoising Autoencoders (DA)**. It can be said that DA is the method that emphasizes the role of equating inputs and outputs. What does this mean? The processing content of DA is as follows: DA adds some noise to input data intentionally and partially damages the data, and then DA performs learning as it restores corrupted data to the original input data. This intentional noise can be easily substantiated if the input data value is [0, 1]; by turning the value of the relevant part into 0 compulsorily. If a data value is out of this range, it can be realized, for example, by adding Gaussian noise, but in this book, we'll think about the former [0, 1] case to understand the core part of the algorithm.

In DA as well, an input/output layer is called a visible layer. DA's graphical model can be shown to be the same shape of RBM, but to get a better understanding, let's follow this diagram:

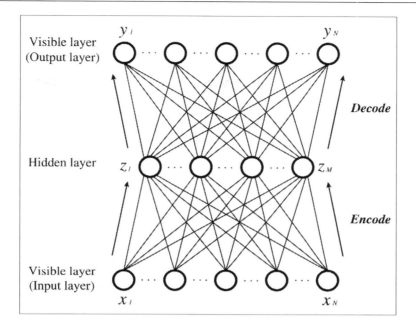

Here, $\tilde{x}$ is the corrupted data, the input data with noise. Then, forward propagation to the hidden layer and the output layer can be represented as follows:

$$z_j = \sigma\left(\sum_{i=1}^{N} w_{ij}\tilde{x}_i + c_j\right)$$

$$y_i = \sigma\left(\sum_{i=1}^{M} w_{ji}z_j + b_i\right)$$

Here, c_j denotes the bias of the hidden layer and b_i the bias of the visible layer. Also, σ denotes the sigmoid function. As seen in the preceding diagram, corrupting input data and mapping to a hidden layer is called **Encode** and mapping to restore the encoded data to the original input data is called **Decode**. Then, DA's evaluation function can be denoted with a negative log likelihood function of the original input data and decoded data:

$$E := -In\,L(\theta) = -\sum_{i=1}^{N}\left\{x_i In\,y_i + (1 - x_i) In(1 - y_i)\right\}$$

Here, θ is the model parameter, the weight and the bias of the visible layer and the hidden layer. What we need to do is just find the gradients of these parameters against the evaluation function. To deform equations easily, we define the functions here:

$$h_j := \sum_{i=1}^{N} w_{ji} \tilde{x}_i + c_j$$

$$g_i := \sum_{j=1}^{M} w_{ji} z_j + b_i$$

Then, we get:

$$z_j = \sigma\left(h_j\right)$$

$$y_i = \sigma\left(g_i\right)$$

Using these functions, each gradient of a parameter can be shown as follows:

$$\frac{\partial E}{\partial w_{ji}} = \frac{\partial E}{\partial h_j} \frac{\partial h_j}{\partial w_{ji}} + \frac{\partial E}{\partial g_i} \frac{\partial g_i}{\partial w_{ji}} = \frac{\partial E}{\partial h_j} \tilde{x}_i + \frac{\partial E}{\partial g_i} z_j$$

$$\frac{\partial E}{\partial b_i} = \frac{\partial E}{\partial g_i} \frac{\partial g_i}{\partial b_i} = \frac{\partial E}{\partial g_i}$$

$$\frac{\partial E}{\partial c_j} = \frac{\partial E}{\partial h_j} \frac{\partial h_j}{\partial c_j} = \frac{\partial E}{\partial h_j}$$

Therefore, only two terms are required. Let's derive them one by one:

$$\frac{\partial E}{\partial h_j} = \frac{\partial E}{\partial z_j}\frac{\partial z_j}{\partial h_j} = \frac{\partial E}{\partial z_j}z_j\left(1-z_j\right)$$

Here, we utilized the derivative of the `sigmoid` function:

$$\frac{d}{dx}\sigma(x) = \sigma(x)\left(1-\sigma(x)\right)$$

Also, we get:

$$\frac{\partial E}{\partial z_j} = \sum_{i=1}^{N}\frac{\partial E}{\partial y_i}\frac{\partial y_i}{\partial z_j}$$

$$= \sum_{i=1}^{N}w_{ji}\left(x_i - y_i\right)$$

Therefore, the following equation can be obtained:

$$\frac{\partial E}{\partial h_j} = \left(\sum_{i=1}^{N}w_{ji}\left(x_i - y_i\right)\right)z_j\left(1-z_j\right)$$

On the other hand, we can also get the following:

$$\frac{\partial E}{\partial g_i} = \frac{\partial E}{\partial y_i}\frac{\partial y_i}{\partial g_i}$$

$$= x_i - y_i$$

Hence, the renewed equation for each parameter will be as follows:

$$w_{ji}^{(k+1)} = w_{ji}^{(k)} + \eta \left[\left(\sum_{i=1}^{N} w_{ji}^{(k)} \left(x_i - y_i \right) \right) z_j \left(1 - z_j \right) \tilde{x}_i + \left(x_i - y_i \right) z_j \right]$$

$$b_i^{(k+1)} = b_i^k + \eta \left(x_i - y_i \right)$$

$$c_j^{(k+1)} = c_j^{(k)} + \eta \left(\sum_{i=1}^{N} w_{ji}^{(k)} \left(x_i - y_i \right) \right) z_j \left(1 - z_j \right)$$

Here, k is the number of iterations and η is the learning rate. Although DA requires a bit of technique for deformation, you can see that the theory itself is very simple compared to RBM.

Now, let's proceed with the implementation. The package structure is the same as the one for RBM.

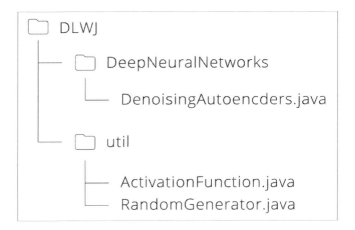

As for model parameters, in addition to the number of units in a hidden layer, the amount of noise being added to the input data is also a parameter in DA. Here, the corruption level is set at 0.3. Generally, this value is often set at $0.1 \sim 0.3$:

```
double corruptionLevel = 0.3;
```

The flow from the building model to training is the same as RBM. Although this method of training is called `contrastiveDivergence` in RBM, it's simply set as `train` in DA:

```
// construct DA
DenoisingAutoencoders nn = new DenoisingAutoencoders(nVisible,
nHidden, null, null, null, rng);

// train
for (int epoch = 0; epoch < epochs; epoch++) {
    for (int batch = 0; batch < minibatch_N; batch++) {
        nn.train(train_X_minibatch[batch], minibatchSize,
        learningRate, corruptionLevel);
    }
}
```

The content of `train` is as explained in the theory section. First of all, add noise to the input data, then encode and decode it:

```
// add noise to original inputs
double[] corruptedInput = getCorruptedInput(X[n], corruptionLevel);

// encode
double[] z = getHiddenValues(corruptedInput);

// decode
double[] y = getReconstructedInput(z);
```

The process of adding noise is, as previously explained, the compulsory turning of the value of the corresponding part of the data into 0:

```
public double[] getCorruptedInput(double[] x, double corruptionLevel)
{

    double[] corruptedInput = new double[x.length];

    // add masking noise
    for (int i = 0; i < x.length; i++) {
        double rand_ = rng.nextDouble();

        if (rand_ < corruptionLevel) {
            corruptedInput[i] = 0.;
        } else {
```

```
                corruptedInput[i] = x[i];
            }
        }

        return corruptedInput;
    }
```

The other processes are just simple activation and propagation, so we won't go through them here. The calculation of the gradients follows math equations:

```
// calculate gradients

// vbias
double[] v_ = new double[nVisible];

for (int i = 0; i < nVisible; i++) {
    v_[i] = X[n][i] - y[i];
    grad_vbias[i] += v_[i];
}

// hbias
double[] h_ = new double[nHidden];

for (int j = 0; j < nHidden; j++) {

    for (int i = 0; i < nVisible; i++) {
        h_[j] = W[j][i] * (X[n][i] - y[i]);
    }

    h_[j] *= z[j] * (1 - z[j]);
    grad_hbias[j] += h_[j];
}

// W
for (int j = 0; j < nHidden; j++) {
    for (int i = 0; i < nVisible; i++) {
        grad_W[j][i] += h_[j] * corruptedInput[i] + v_[i] * z[j];
    }
}
```

Compared to RBM, the implementation of DA is also quite simple. When you test (`reconstruct`) the model, you don't need to corrupt the data. As in standard neural networks, you just need to forward propagate the given inputs based on the weights of the networks:

```
public double[] reconstruct(double[] x) {

    double[] z = getHiddenValues(x);
    double[] y = getReconstructedInput(z);

    return y;
}
```

Stacked Denoising Autoencoders (SDA)

SDA is deep neural networks with piled up DA layers. In the same way that DBN consists of RBMs and logistic regression, SDA consists of DAs and logistic regression:

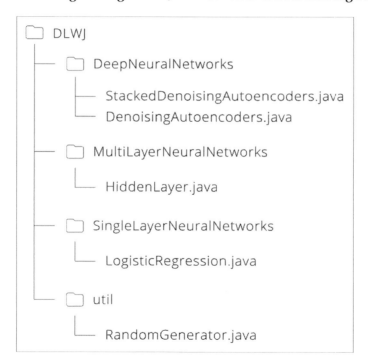

The flow of implementation is not that different between DBN and SDA. Even though there is a difference between RBM and DA in pre-training, the content of fine-tuning is exactly the same. Therefore, not much explanation might be needed.

The method for pre-training is not that different, but please note that the point where the `int` type was used for DBN is changed to double type, as DA can handle `[0, 1]`, not binary:

```
public void pretrain(double[][][] X, int minibatchSize, int
minibatch_N, int epochs, double learningRate, double
corruptionLevel) {

    for (int layer = 0; layer < nLayers; layer++) {
        for (int epoch = 0; epoch < epochs; epoch++) {
            for (int batch = 0; batch < minibatch_N; batch++) {

                double[][] X_ = new double[minibatchSize][nIn];
                double[][] prevLayerX_;

                // Set input data for current layer
                if (layer == 0) {
                    X_ = X[batch];
                } else {

                    prevLayerX_ = X_;
                    X_ = new
                    double[minibatchSize][hiddenLayerSizes[layer-1]];

                    for (int i = 0; i < minibatchSize; i++) {
                        X_[i] = sigmoidLayers[layer-
                        1].output(prevLayerX_[i]);
                    }
                }

                daLayers[layer].train(X_, minibatchSize,
                learningRate, corruptionLevel);
            }
        }
    }

}
```

The `predict` method after learning is also exactly the same as in DBN. Considering that both DBN and SDA can be treated as one multi-layer neural network after learning (that is, the pre-training and fine-tuning), it's natural that most of the processes are common.

Overall, SDA can be implemented more easily than DBN, but the precision to be obtained is almost the same. This is the merit of SDA.

Summary

In this chapter, we looked at the problem of the previous neural networks algorithm and what the breakthrough was for deep learning. Also, you learned about the theory and implementation of DBN and SDA, the algorithm that fueled the boom of deep learning, and of RBM and DA used in each respective method.

In the next chapter, we'll look at more deep learning algorithms. They take different approaches to obtain high precision rates and are well developed.

4
Dropout and Convolutional Neural Networks

In this chapter, we continue to look through the algorithms of deep learning. The pre-training that was taken into both DBN and SDA is indeed an innovative method, but deep learning also has other innovative methods. Among these methods, we'll go into the details of the particularly eminent algorithms, which are the following:

- The dropout learning algorithm
- Convolutional neural networks

Both algorithms are necessary to understand and master deep learning, so make sure you keep up.

Deep learning algorithms without pre-training

In the previous chapter, you learned that layer-wise training with pre-training was a breakthrough for DBN and SDA. The reason why these algorithms need pre-training is because an issue occurs where an output error gradually vanishes and doesn't work well in neural networks with simple piled-up layers (we call this the vanishing gradient problem). The deep learning algorithm needs pre-training whether you want to improve the existing method or reinvent it—you might think of it like that.

However, actually, the deep learning algorithms in this chapter don't have a phase of pre-training, albeit in the deep learning algorithm without pre-training, we can get a result with higher precision and accuracy. Why is such a thing possible? Here is a brief reason. Let's think about why the vanishing gradient problem occurs — remember the equation of backpropagation? A delta in a layer is distributed to all the units of a previous layer by literally propagating networks backward. This means that in the network where all units are tied densely, the value of an error backpropagated to each unit becomes small. As you can see from the equations of backpropagation, the gradients of the weight are obtained by the multiplication of the weights and deltas among the units. Hence, the more terms we have, the more dense the networks are and the more possibilities we have for underflow. This causes the vanishing gradient problem.

Therefore, we can say that if the preceding problems can be avoided without pre-training, a machine can learn properly with deep neural networks. To achieve this, we need to arrange how to connect the networks. The deep learning algorithm in this chapter is a method that puts this contrivance into practice using various approaches.

Dropout

If there's a problem with the network being tied densely, just force it to be sparse. Then the vanishing gradient problem won't occur and learning can be done properly. The algorithm based on such an idea is the **dropout** algorithm. Dropout for deep neural networks was introduced in *Improving neural networks by preventing co adaptation of feature detectors* (Hinton, et. al. 2012, http://arxiv. org/pdf/1207.0580.pdf) and refined in *Dropout: A Simple Way to Prevent Neural Networks from Overfitting* (Srivastava, et. al. 2014, https://www.cs.toronto. edu/~hinton/absps/JMLRdropout.pdf). In dropout, some of the units are, literally, forcibly dropped while training. What does this mean? Let's look at the following figures — firstly, neural networks:

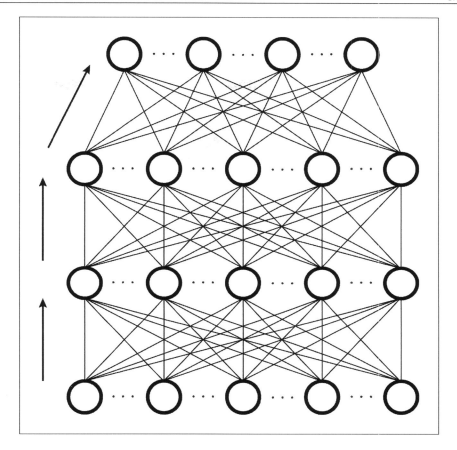

There is nothing special about this figure. It is a standard neural network with one input layer, two hidden layers, and one output layer. Secondly, the graphical model can be represented as follows by applying dropout to this network:

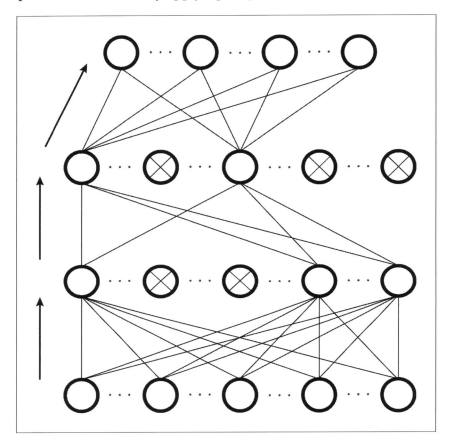

Units that are dropped from the network are depicted with cross signs. As you can see in the preceding figure, dropped units are interpreted as non-existent in the network. This means we need to change the structure of the original neural network while the dropout learning algorithm is being applied. Thankfully, applying dropout to the network is not difficult from a computational standpoint. You can simply build a general deep neural network first. Then the dropout learning algorithm can be applied just by adding a dropout mask—a simple binary mask—to all the units in each layer. Units with the value of 0 in the binary mask are the ones that are dropped from the network.

This may remind you of DA (or SDA) discussed in the previous chapter because DA and dropout look similar at first glance. Corrupting input data in DA also adds binary masks to the data when implemented. However, there are two remarkably different points between them. First, while it is true that both methods have the process of adding masks to neurons, DA applies the mask only to units in the input layer, whereas dropout applies it to units in the hidden layer. Some of the dropout algorithms apply masks to both the input layer and the hidden layer, but this is still different from DA. Second, in DA, once the corrupt input data is generated, the data will be used throughout the whole training epochs, but in dropout, the data with different masks will be used in each training epoch. This indicates that a neural network of a different shape is trained in each iteration. Dropout masks will be generated in each layer in each iteration according to the probability of dropout.

You might have a question—can we train the model even if the shape of the network is different in every step? The answer is yes. You can think of it this way—the network is well trained with dropout because it puts more weights on the existing neurons to reflect the characteristics of the input data. However, dropout has a single demerit, that is, it requires more training epochs than other algorithms to train and optimize the model, which means it takes more time until it is optimized. Another technique is introduced here to reduce this problem. Although the dropout algorithm itself was invented earlier, it was not enough for deep neural networks to gain the ability to generalize and get high precision rates just by using this method. With one more technique that makes the network even more sparse, we achieve deep neural networks to get higher accuracy. This technique is the improvement of the activation function, which we can say is a simple yet elegant solution.

All of the methods of neural networks explained so far utilize the sigmoid function or hyperbolic tangent as an activation function. You might get great results with these functions. However, as you can see from the shape of them, these curves saturate and kill the gradients when the input values or error values at a certain layer are relatively large or small.

One of the activation functions introduced to solve this problem is the **rectifier**. A unit-applied rectifier is called a **Rectified Linear Unit (ReLU)**. We can call the activation function itself ReLU. This function is described in the following equation:

$$f(x) = \max(0, x) = \begin{cases} x & \text{if } x \geq 0 \\ 0 & \text{otherwise} \end{cases}$$

The function can be represented by the following figure:

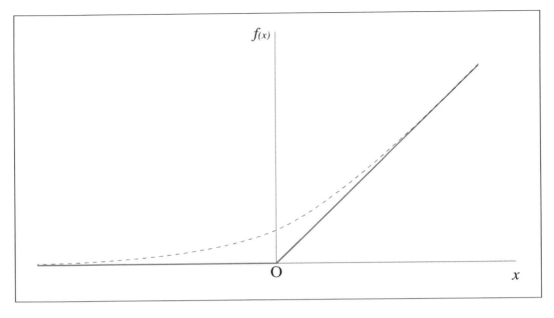

The broken line in the figure is the function called a **softplus function**, the derivative of it is logistic function, which can be described as follows:

$$softplus(x) = in(1 + \exp(x))$$

This is just for your information: we have the following relations that a smooth approximation to the rectifier. As you can see from the figure above, since the rectifier is far simpler than the sigmoid function and hyperbolic tangent, you can easily guess that the time cost will reduce when it is applied to the deep learning algorithm. In addition, because the derivative of the rectifier—which is necessary when calculating backpropagation errors—is also simple, we can, additionally, shorten the time cost. The equation of the derivative can be represented as follows:

$$f'(x) = \begin{cases} 1 & if\ x \geq 0 \\ 0 & otherwise \end{cases}$$

Since both the rectifier and the derivative of it are very sparse, we can easily imagine that the neural networks will be also sparse through training. You may have also noticed that we no longer have to worry about gradient saturations because we don't have the causal curves that the sigmoid function and hyperbolic tangent contain anymore.

With the technique of dropout and the rectifier, a simple deep neural network can learn a problem without pre-training. In terms of the equations used to implement the dropout algorithm, they are not difficult because they are just simple methods of adding dropout masks to multi-layer perceptrons. Let's look at them in order:

$$Z_j = h\left(\sum_i w_{ji}x_i + b_j \right)$$

Here, $h(\cdot)$ denotes the activation function, which is, in this case, the rectifier. You see, the previous equation is for units in the hidden layer without dropout. What the dropout does is just apply the mask to them. It can be represented as follows:

$$Zj = h\left(\sum_i w_{ji}x_i + b_j \right) m_j$$

$$m_j \sim Bernoulli\left(1 - p\right)$$

Here, p denotes the probability of dropout, which is generally set to 0.5. That's all for forward activation. As you can see from the equations, the term of the binary mask is the only difference from the ones of general neural networks. In addition, during backpropagation, we also have to add masks to the delta. Suppose we have the following equation:

$$a_j = \sum_i w_{ji}x_i + b_j$$

With this, we can define the delta as follows:

$$\delta_j := \frac{\partial E_n}{\partial a_j} = \sum_k \frac{\partial E_n}{\partial a_k}\frac{\partial a_k}{\partial a_j}$$

Here, E_n denotes the evaluation function (these equations are the same as we mentioned in *Chapter 2, Algorithms for Machine Learning – Preparing for Deep Learning*). We get the following equation:

$$a_k = \sum_j w_{kj}z_j + c_k$$
$$= \sum_j w_{kj}h\big(a_j\big)m_j + c_k$$

Here, the delta can be described as follows:

$$\delta_j = h'\big(a_j\big)m_j\sum_k \delta_k w_{kj}$$

Now we have all the equations necessary for implementation, let's dive into the implementation. The package structure is as follows:

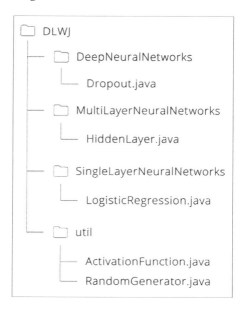

First, what we need to have is the rectifier. Like other activation functions, we implement it in `ActivationFunction.java` as ReLU:

```java
public static double ReLU(double x) {
    if(x > 0) {
        return x;
    } else {
        return 0.;
    }
}
```

Also, we define dReLU as the derivative of the rectifier:

```java
public static double dReLU(double y) {
    if(y > 0) {
        return 1.;
    } else {
        return 0.;
    }
}
```

Accordingly, we updated the constructor of `HiddenLayer.java` to support ReLU:

```java
if (activation == "sigmoid" || activation == null) {

    this.activation = (double x) -> sigmoid(x);
    this.dactivation = (double x) -> dsigmoid(x);

} else if (activation == "tanh") {

    this.activation = (double x) -> tanh(x);
    this.dactivation = (double x) -> dtanh(x);

} else if (activation == "ReLU") {

    this.activation = (double x) -> ReLU(x);
    this.dactivation = (double x) -> dReLU(x);

} else {
    throw new IllegalArgumentException("activation function not
supported");
}
```

Now let's have a look at `Dropout.java`. In the source code, we'll build the neural networks of two hidden layers, and the probability of dropout is set to 0.5:

```
int[] hiddenLayerSizes = {100, 80};
double pDropout = 0.5;
```

The constructor of `Dropout.java` can be written as follows (since the network is just a simple deep neural network, the code is also simple):

```
public Dropout(int nIn, int[] hiddenLayerSizes, int nOut, Random rng,
String activation) {

    if (rng == null) rng = new Random(1234);

    if (activation == null) activation = "ReLU";

    this.nIn = nIn;
    this.hiddenLayerSizes = hiddenLayerSizes;
    this.nOut = nOut;
    this.nLayers = hiddenLayerSizes.length;
    this.hiddenLayers = new HiddenLayer[nLayers];
    this.rng = rng;

    // construct multi-layer
    for (int i = 0; i < nLayers; i++) {
        int nIn_;
        if (i == 0) nIn_ = nIn;
        else nIn_ = hiddenLayerSizes[i - 1];

        // construct hidden layer
        hiddenLayers[i] = new HiddenLayer(nIn_,
        hiddenLayerSizes[i], null, null, rng, activation);
    }

    // construct logistic layer
    logisticLayer = new LogisticRegression(hiddenLayerSizes[nLayers -
1], nOut);
}
```

As explained, now we have the `HiddenLayer` class with `ReLU` support, we can use `ReLU` as the activation function.

Once a model is built, what we do next is train the model with dropout. The method for training is simply called `train`. Since we need some layer inputs when calculating the backpropagation errors, we define the variable called `layerInputs` first to cache their respective input values:

```
List<double[][]> layerInputs = new ArrayList<>(nLayers+1);
layerInputs.add(X);
```

Here, x is the original training data. We also need to cache the dropout masks for each layer for backpropagation, so let's define it as `dropoutMasks`:

```
List<int[][]> dropoutMasks = new ArrayList<>(nLayers);
```

Training begins in a forward activation fashion. Look how we apply the dropout masks to the value; we merely multiply the activated values and binary masks:

```
// forward hidden layers
for (int layer = 0; layer < nLayers; layer++) {

    double[] x_;  // layer input
    double[][] Z_ = new
    double[minibatchSize][hiddenLayerSizes[layer]];
    int[][] mask_ = new
    int[minibatchSize][hiddenLayerSizes[layer]];

    for (int n = 0; n < minibatchSize; n++) {

        if (layer == 0) {
            x_ = X[n];
        } else {
            x_ = Z[n];
        }


        Z_[n] = hiddenLayers[layer].forward(x_);
        mask_[n] = dropout(Z_[n], pDrouput);  // apply dropout mask
        to units
    }

    Z = Z_;
    layerInputs.add(Z.clone());

    dropoutMasks.add(mask_);
}
```

The dropout method is defined in `Dropout.java` as well. As explained in the equation, this method returns the values following the Bernoulli distribution:

```
public int[] dropout(double[] z, double p) {

    int size = z.length;
    int[] mask = new int[size];

    for (int i = 0; i < size; i++) {
        mask[i] = binomial(1, 1 - p, rng);
        z[i] *= mask[i]; // apply mask
    }

    return mask;
}
```

After forward propagation through the hidden layers, training data is forward propagated in the output layer of the logistic regression. Then, in the same way as the other neural networks algorithm, the deltas of each layer are going back through the network. Here, we apply the cached masks to the delta so that its values are backpropagated in the same network:

```
// forward & backward output layer
D = logisticLayer.train(Z, T, minibatchSize, learningRate);

// backward hidden layers
for (int layer = nLayers - 1; layer >= 0; layer--) {

    double[][] Wprev_;

    if (layer == nLayers - 1) {
        Wprev_ = logisticLayer.W;
    } else {
        Wprev_ = hiddenLayers[layer+1].W;
    }

    // apply mask to delta as well
    for (int n = 0; n < minibatchSize; n++) {
        int[] mask_ = dropoutMasks.get(layer)[n];

        for (int j = 0; j < D[n].length; j++) {
            D[n][j] *= mask_[j];
```

```
        }
    }

    D = hiddenLayers[layer].backward(layerInputs.get(layer),
    layerInputs.get(layer+1), D, Wprev_, minibatchSize,
    learningRate);
}
```

After the training comes the test phase. But before we apply the test data to the tuned model, we need to configure the weights of the network. Dropout masks can't be simply applied to the test data because when masked, the shape of each network will be differentiated, and this may return different results because a certain unit may have a significant effect on certain features. Instead, what we do is smooth the weights of the network, which means we simulate the network where whole units are equally masked. This can be done using the following equation:

$$W_{test} = (1 - p)W$$

As you can see from the equation, all the weights are multiplied by the probability of non-dropout. We define the method for this as `pretest`:

```
public void pretest(double pDropout) {

    for (int layer = 0; layer < nLayers; layer++) {

        int nIn_, nOut_;

        if (layer == 0) {
            nIn_ = nIn;
        } else {
            nIn_ = hiddenLayerSizes[layer];
        }

        if (layer == nLayers - 1) {
            nOut_ = nOut;
        } else {
            nOut_ = hiddenLayerSizes[layer+1];
        }

        for (int j = 0; j < nOut_; j++) {
            for (int i = 0; i < nIn_; i++) {
                hiddenLayers[layer].W[j][i] *= 1 - pDropout;
            }
        }
    }
}
```

We have to call this method once before the test. Since the network is a general multi-layered neural network, what we need to do for the prediction is just perform forward activation through the network:

```java
public Integer[] predict(double[] x) {

    double[] z = new double[0];

    for (int layer = 0; layer < nLayers; layer++) {

        double[] x_;

        if (layer == 0) {
            x_ = x;
        } else {
            x_ = z.clone();
        }

        z = hiddenLayers[layer].forward(x_);
    }

    return logisticLayer.predict(z);
}
```

Compared to DBN and SDA, the dropout MLP is far simpler and easier to implement. It suggests the possibility that with a mixture of two or more techniques, we can get higher precision.

Convolutional neural networks

All the machine learning/deep learning algorithms you have learned about imply that the type of input data is one-dimensional. When you look at a real-world application, however, data is not necessarily one-dimensional. A typical case is an image. Though we can still convert two-dimensional (or higher-dimensional) data into a one-dimensional array from the standpoint of implementation, it would be better to build a model that can handle two-dimensional data as it is. Otherwise, some information embedded in the data, such as positional relationships, might be lost when flattened to one dimension.

To solve this problem, an algorithm called **Convolutional Neural Networks (CNN)** was proposed. In CNN, features are extracted from two-dimensional input data through convolutional layers and pooling layers (this will be explained later), and then these features are put into general multi-layer perceptrons. This preprocessing for MLP is inspired by human visual areas and can be described as follows:

- Segment the input data into several domains. This process is equivalent to a human's receptive fields.

- Extract the features from the respective domains, such as edges and position aberrations.

With these features, MLP can classify data accordingly.

The graphical model of CNN is not similar to that of other neural networks. Here is a briefly outlined example of CNN:

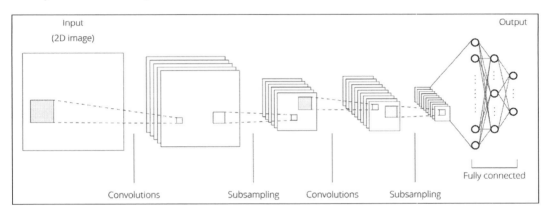

You may not fully understand what CNN is just from the figure. Moreover, you might feel that CNN is relatively complicated and difficult to understand. But you don't have to worry about that. It is a fact that CNN has a complicated graphical model and has unfamiliar terminologies such as convolution and pooling, which you don't hear about in other deep learning algorithms. However, when you look at the model step by step, there's nothing too difficult to understand. CNN consists of several types of layers specifically adjusted for image recognition. Let's look at each layer one by one in the next subsection. In the preceding figure, there are two convolution and pooling (**Subsampling**) layers and fully connected multi-layer perceptrons in the network. We'll see what the convolutional layers do first.

Convolution

Convolutional layers literally perform convolution, which means applying several filters to the image to extract features. These filters are called **kernels**, and convolved images are called **feature maps**. Let's see the following image (decomposed to color values) and kernel:

Image						Kernel		
1	0	0	1	1		1	0	1
0	1	1	1	0		0	1	0
1	1	1	0	1		1	0	1
0	1	0	1	1				
1	0	0	1	1				

With these, what is done with convolution is illustrated as follows:

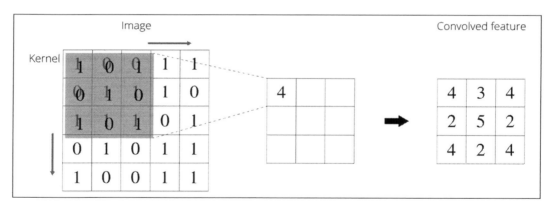

The kernel slides across the image and returns the summation of its values within the kernel as a multiplication filter. You might have noticed that you can extract many kinds of features by changing kernel values. Suppose you have kernels with values as described here:

-1	-1	-1		0.1	0.1	0.1
-1	8	-1		0.1	0.1	0.1
-1	-1	-1		0.1	0.1	0.1

You see that the kernel on the left extracts the edges of the image because it accentuates the color differences, and the one on the right blurs the image because it degrades the original values. The great thing about CNN is that in convolutional layers, you don't have to set these kernel values manually. Once initialized, CNN itself will learn the proper values through the learning algorithm (which means parameters trained in CNN are the weights of kernels) and can classify images very precisely in the end.

Now, let's think about why neural networks with convolutional layers (kernels) can predict with higher precision rates. The key here is the **local receptive field**. In most layers in neural networks except CNN, all neurons are fully connected. This even causes slightly different data, for example, one-pixel parallel data would be regarded as completely different data in the network because this data is propagated to different neurons in hidden layers, whereas humans can easily understand they are the same. With fully connected layers, it is true that neural networks can recognize more complicated patterns, but at the same time they lack the ability to generalize and lack flexibility. In contrast, you can see that connections among neurons in convolutional layers are limited to their kernel size, making the model more robust to translated images. Thus, neural networks with their receptive fields limited locally are able to acquire **translation invariance** when kernels are optimized.

Each kernel has its own values and extracts respective features from the image. Please bear in mind that the number of feature maps and the number of kernels are always the same, which means if we have 20 kernels, we have also twenty feature maps, that is, convolved images. This can be confusing, so let's explore another example. Given a gray-scaled **image** and twenty **kernels**, how many **feature maps** are there? The answer is twenty. These twenty images will be propagated to the next layer. This is illustrated as follows:

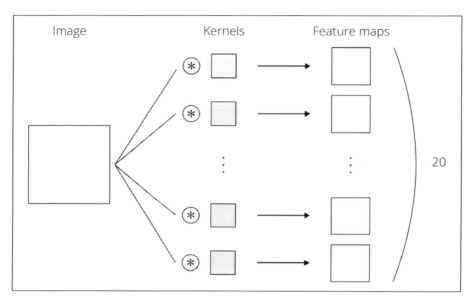

So, how about this: suppose we have a 3-channeled image (for example, an RGB image) and the number of kernels is twenty, how many feature maps will there be? The answer is, again, twenty. But this time, the process of convolution is different from the one with gray-scaled, that is 1-channeled, images. When the image has multiple channels, kernels will be adapted separately for each channel. Therefore, in this case, we will have a total of 60 convolved images first, composed of twenty mapped images for each of the 3 channels. Then, all the convolved images originally from the same image will be combined into one feature map. As a result, we will have twenty feature maps. In other words, images are decomposed into different channeled data, applied kernels, and then combined into mixed-channeled images again. You can easily imagine from the flow in the preceding diagram that when we apply a kernel to a multi-channeled image to make decomposed images, the same kernel should be applied. This flow can be seen in the following figure:

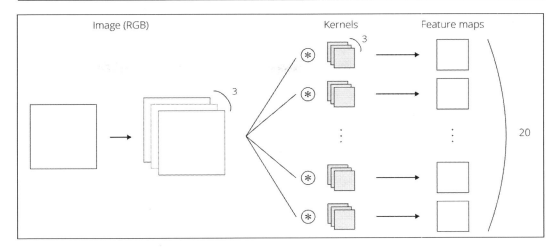

Computationally, the number of kernels is represented with the dimension of the weights' tensor. You'll see how to implement this later.

Pooling

What pooling layers do is rather simple compared to convolutional layers. They actually do not train or learn by themselves but just downsample images propagated from convolutional layers. Why should we bother to do downsampling? You might think it may lose some significant information from the data. But here, again, as with convolutional layers, this process is necessary to make the network keep its translation invariance.

There are several ways of downsampling, but among them, max-pooling is the most famous. It can be represented as follows:

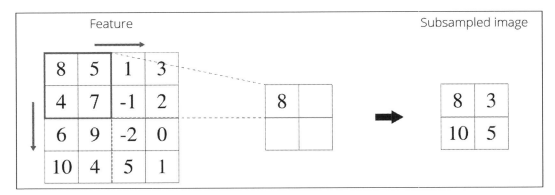

In a max-pooling layer, the input image is segmented into a set of non-overlapping sub-data and the maximum value is output from each data. This process not only keeps its translation invariance but also reduces the computation for the upper layers. With convolution and pooling, CNN can acquire robust features from the input.

Equations and implementations

Now we know what convolution and max-pooling are, let's describe the whole model with equations. We'll use the figure of convolution below in equations:

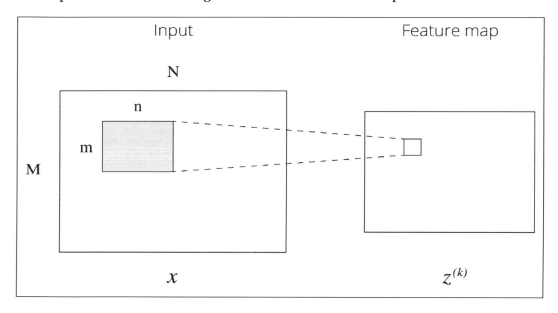

As shown in the figure, if we have an image with a size of $M \times N$ and kernels with a size of $m \times n$, the convolution can be represented as:

$$z_{ij}^{(k)} = \sum_{s=0}^{m-1} \sum_{t=0}^{n-1} w_{st}^{(k)} x(i+s)(j+t)$$

Here, w is the weight of the kernel, that is, the model parameter. Just bear in mind we've described each summation from 0, not from 1, so you get a better understanding. The equation, however, is not enough when we think about multi-convolutional layers because it does not have the information from the channel. Fortunately, it's not difficult because we can implement it just by adding one parameter to the kernel. The extended equation can be shown as:

$$z_{ij}^{(k)} = \sum_{c} \sum_{s=0}^{m-1} \sum_{t=0}^{n-1} w_{st}^{(k,c)} x_{(i+s)(j+t)}^{(c)}$$

Here, c denotes the channel of the image. If the number of kernels is K and the number of channels is C, we have $W \in \mathbb{R}^{K \times C \times m \times n}$. Then, you can see from the equation that the size of the convolved image is $(M - m + 1) \times (N - n + 1)$.

After the convolution, all the convolved values will be activated by the activation function. We'll implement CNN with the rectifier — the most popular function these days — but you may use the sigmoid function, the hyperbolic tangent, or any other activation functions available instead. With the activation, we have:

$$a_{ij}^{(k)} = h\left(z_{ij}^{(k)} + b^{(k)}\right) = \max\left(0, z_{ij}^{(k)} + b^{(k)}\right)$$

Here, b denotes the bias, the other model parameter. You can see that b doesn't have subscripts of i and j, that is, we have $b \in \mathbb{R}^{K}$, a one-dimensional array. Thus, we have forward-propagated the values of the convolutional layer.

Next comes the max-pooling layer. The propagation can simply be written as follows:

$$y_{ij}^{(k)} = \max\left(a_{(l_1 i + s)(l_2 j + t)}^{(k)}\right)$$

Here, l_1 and l_2 are the size of pooling filter and $s \in [0, l_1], t \in [0, l_2]$. Usually, l_1 and l_2 are set to the same value of 2 ~ 4.

These two layers, the convolutional layer and the max-pooling layer, tend to be arrayed in this order, but you don't necessarily have to follow it. You can put two convolutional layers before max-pooling, for example. Also, while we put the activation right after the convolution, sometimes it is set after the max-pooling instead of the convolution. For simplicity, however, we'll implement CNN with the order and sequence of convolution–activation–max-pooling.

[One important note here is that although the kernel weights will be learned from the data, the architecture, the size of kernel, and the size of pooling are all parameters.]

The simple MLP follows after convolutional layers and max-pooling layers to classify the data. Here, since MLP can only accept one-dimensional data, we need to flatten the downsampled data as preprocessing to adapt it to the input layer of MLP. The extraction of features was completed before MLP, so formatting the data into one dimension won't be a problem. Thus, CNN can classify the image data once the model is optimized. To do this, as with other neural networks, the backpropagation algorithm is applied to CNN to train the model. We won't mention the equation related to MLP here.

The error from the input layer of MLP is backpropagated to the max-pooling layer, and this time it is unflattened to two dimensions to be adapted properly to the model. Since the max-pooling layer doesn't have model parameters, it simply backpropagates the error to the previous layer. The equation can be described as follows:

$$
\frac{\partial E}{\partial a^{(k)}_{(l_1 i+s)(l_2 j+t)}} = \begin{cases} \dfrac{\partial E}{\partial y^{(k)}_{ij}} & if \ y^{(k)}_{ij} = a^{(k)}_{(l_1 i+s)(l_2 j+t)} \\ 0 & otherwise \end{cases}
$$

Here, E denotes the evaluation function. This error is then backpropagated to the convolutional layer, and with it we can calculate the gradients of the weight and the bias. Since the activation with the bias comes before the convolution when backpropagating, let's see the gradient of the bias first, as follows:

$$
\frac{\partial E}{\partial b^{(k)}} = \sum_{i=0}^{M-m} \sum_{j=0}^{N-m} \frac{\partial E}{\partial a^{(k)}_{ij}} \frac{\partial a^{(k)}_{ij}}{\partial b^{(k)}}
$$

To proceed with this equation, we define the following:

$$\delta_{ij}^{(k)} := \frac{\partial E}{\partial a_{ij}^{(k)}}$$

We also define:

$$c_{ij}^{(k)} := z_{ij}^{(k)} + b^{(k)}$$

With these, we get:

$$\frac{\partial E}{\partial b^{(k)}} = \sum_{i=0}^{M-m} \sum_{j=0}^{N-n} \delta_{ij}^{(k)} \frac{\partial a_{ij}^{(k)}}{\partial c_{ij}^{(k)}} \frac{\partial c_j^{(k)}}{\partial b_{(k)}}$$

$$= \sum_{i=0}^{M-m} \sum_{j=0}^{N-n} \delta_{ij}^{(k)} h'\left(c_{ij}^{(k)}\right)$$

We can calculate the gradient of the weight (kernel) in the same way:

$$\frac{\partial E}{\partial w_{st}^{(k,c)}} = \sum_{i=0}^{M-m} \sum_{j=0}^{N-n} \frac{\partial E}{\partial z_{ij}^{(k)}} \frac{\partial z_{ij}^{(k)}}{\partial w_{st}^{(k,c)}}$$

$$= \sum_{i=0}^{M-m} \sum_{j=0}^{N-n} \frac{\partial E}{\partial z_{ij}^{(k)}} \frac{\partial a_{ij}^{(k)}}{\partial z_{ij}^{(k)}} x_{(i+s)(j+t)}^{(c)}$$

$$= \sum_{i=0}^{M-m} \sum_{j=0}^{N-n} \delta_{ij}^{(k)} h'\left(c_{ij}^{(k)}\right) x_{(i+s)(j+t)}^{(c)}$$

Thus, we can update the model parameters. If we have just one convolutional and max-pooling layer, the equations just given are all that we need. When we think of multi-convolutional layers, however, we also need to calculate the error of the convolutional layers. This can be represented as follows:

$$\frac{\partial E}{\partial w_{ij}^{(c)}} = \sum_{k}\sum_{s=0}^{m-1}\sum_{t=0}^{n-1} \frac{\partial E}{\partial z_{(i-s)(j-t)}^{(k)}} \frac{\partial z_{(i-s)(j-t)}^{(k)}}{\partial x_{ij}^{(c)}}$$

$$= \sum_{k}\sum_{s=0}^{m-1}\sum_{t=0}^{n-1} \frac{\partial E}{\partial z_{(i-s)(j-t)}^{(k)}} w_{st}^{(k,c)}$$

Here, we get:

$$\frac{\partial E}{\partial z_{ij}^{(c)}} = \frac{\partial E}{\partial a_{ij}^{(k)}} \frac{\partial a_{ij}^{(k)}}{\partial z_{ij}^{(k)}}$$

$$= \delta_{ij}^{(k)} \frac{\partial a_{ij}^{(k)}}{\partial c_{ij}^{(k)}} \frac{\partial c_{ij}^{(k)}}{\partial z_{ij}^{(k)}}$$

$$= \delta_{ij}^{(k)} h'\left(c_{ij}^{(k)}\right)$$

So, the error can be written as follows:

$$\frac{\partial E}{\partial x_{ij}^{(c)}} = \sum_{k}\sum_{s=0}^{m-1}\sum_{t=0}^{n-1} \delta_{(i-s)(j-t)}^{(k)} h'\left(c_{(i-s)(j-t)}^{(k)}\right) w_{st}^{(k,c)}$$

We have to be careful when calculating this because there's a possibility of $i - s < 0$ or $j - t < 0$, where there's no element in between the feature maps. To solve this, we need to add zero paddings to the top-left edges of them. Then, the equation is simply a convolution with the kernel flipped along both axes. Though the equations in CNN might look complicated, they are just a pile of summations of each parameter.

With all the previous equations, we can now implement CNN, so let's see how we do it. The package structure is as follows:

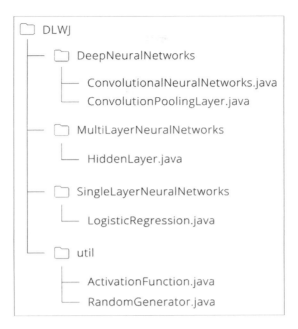

`ConvolutionNeuralNetworks.java` is used to build the model outline of CNN, and the exact algorithms for training in the convolutional layers and max-pooling layers, forward propagations, and backpropagations are written in `ConvolutionPoolingLayer.java`. In the demo, we have the original image size of 12×12 with one channel:

```
final int[] imageSize = {12, 12};
final int channel = 1;
```

The image will be propagated through two `ConvPoolingLayer` (convolutional layers and max-pooling layers). The number of kernels in the first layer is set to 10 with the size of 3×3 and 20 with the size of 2×2 in the second layer. The size of the pooling filters are both set to 2×2:

```
int[] nKernels = {10, 20};
int[][] kernelSizes = { {3, 3}, {2, 2} };
int[][] poolSizes = { {2, 2}, {2, 2} };
```

After the second max-pooling layer, there are 20 feature maps with the size of 2 × 2. These maps are then flattened to 80 units and will be forwarded to the hidden layer with 20 neurons:

```
int nHidden = 20;
```

We then create simple demo data of three patterns with a little noise. We'll leave out the code to create demo data here. If we illustrate the data, here is an example of it:

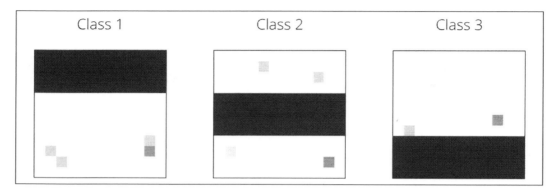

Now let's build the model. The constructor is similar to other deep learning models and rather simple. We construct multi `ConvolutionPoolingLayers` first. The size for each layer is calculated in the method:

```
// construct convolution + pooling layers
for (int i = 0; i < nKernels.length; i++) {
    int[] size_;
    int channel_;

    if (i == 0) {
        size_ = new int[]{imageSize[0], imageSize[1]};
        channel_ = channel;
    } else {
        size_ = new int[]{pooledSizes[i-1][0], pooledSizes[i-
        1][1]};
        channel_ = nKernels[i-1];
    }

    convolvedSizes[i] = new int[]{size_[0] - kernelSizes[i][0] + 1,
    size_[1] - kernelSizes[i][1] + 1};
```

```
        pooledSizes[i] = new int[]{convolvedSizes[i][0] /
        poolSizes[i][0], convolvedSizes[i][1] / poolSizes[i][0]};

        convpoolLayers[i] = new ConvolutionPoolingLayer(size_,
        channel_, nKernels[i], kernelSizes[i], poolSizes[i],
        convolvedSizes[i], pooledSizes[i], rng, activation);
    }
```

When you look at the constructor of the ConvolutionPoolingLayer class, you can see how the kernel and the bias are defined:

```
if (W == null) {

    W = new double[nKernel][channel][kernelSize[0]][kernelSize[1]];

    double in_ = channel * kernelSize[0] * kernelSize[1];
    double out_ = nKernel * kernelSize[0] * kernelSize[1] /
    (poolSize[0] * poolSize[1]);
    double w_ = Math.sqrt(6. / (in_ + out_));

    for (int k = 0; k < nKernel; k++) {
        for (int c = 0; c < channel; c++) {
            for (int s = 0; s < kernelSize[0]; s++) {
                for (int t = 0; t < kernelSize[1]; t++) {
                    W[k][c][s][t] = uniform(-w_, w_, rng);
                }
            }
        }
    }
}

if (b == null) b = new double[nKernel];
```

Next comes the construction of MLP. Don't forget to flatten the downsampled data when passing through them:

```
// build MLP
flattenedSize = nKernels[nKernels.length-1] * pooledSizes[pooledSizes.
length-1][0] * pooledSizes[pooledSizes.length-1][1];

// construct hidden layer
hiddenLayer = new HiddenLayer(flattenedSize, nHidden, null, null, rng,
activation);

// construct output layer
logisticLayer = new LogisticRegression(nHidden, nOut);
```

Once the model is built, we need to train it. In the `train` method, we cache all the forward-propagated data so that we can utilize it when backpropagating:

```
// cache pre-activated, activated, and downsampled inputs of each
convolution + pooling layer for backpropagation
List<double[][][][]> preActivated_X = new ArrayList<>(nKernels.
length);
List<double[][][][]> activated_X = new ArrayList<>(nKernels.length);
List<double[][][][]> downsampled_X = new ArrayList<>(nKernels.
length+1);  // +1 for input X
downsampled_X.add(X);

for (int i = 0; i < nKernels.length; i++) {
   preActivated_X.add(new
   double[minibatchSize][nKernels[i]][convolvedSizes[i][0]]
   [convolvedSizes[i][1]]);
   activated_X.add(new
   double[minibatchSize][nKernels[i]][convolvedSizes[i][0]]
   [convolvedSizes[i][1]]);
   downsampled_X.add(new
   double[minibatchSize][nKernels[i]][convolvedSizes[i][0]]
   [convolvedSizes[i][1]]);
}
```

`preActivated_X` is defined for convolved feature maps, `activated_X` for activated features, and `downsampled_X` for downsampled features. We put and cache the original data into `downsampled_X`. The actual training begins with forward propagation through convolution and max-pooling:

```
// forward convolution + pooling layers
double[][][] z_ = X[n].clone();
for (int i = 0; i < nKernels.length; i++) {
   z_ = convpoolLayers[i].forward(z_, preActivated_X.get(i)[n],
   activated_X.get(i)[n]);
   downsampled_X.get(i+1)[n] = z_.clone();
}
```

The `forward` method of `ConvolutionPoolingLayer` is simple and consists of `convolve` and `downsample`. The `convolve` function does the convolution, and `downsample` does the max-pooling:

```
public double[][][] forward(double[][][] x, double[][][]
preActivated_X, double[][][] activated_X) {

   double[][][] z = this.convolve(x, preActivated_X, activated_X);
   return  this.downsample(z);
```

The values of `preActivated_X` and `activated_X` are set inside the convolve method. You can see that the method simply follows the equations explained previously:

```java
public double[][][] convolve(double[][][] x, double[][][]
preActivated_X, double[][][] activated_X) {

    double[][][] y = new
    double[nKernel][convolvedSize[0]][convolvedSize[1]];

    for (int k = 0; k < nKernel; k++) {
        for (int i = 0; i < convolvedSize[0]; i++) {
            for(int j = 0; j < convolvedSize[1]; j++) {

                double convolved_ = 0.;

                for (int c = 0; c < channel; c++) {
                    for (int s = 0; s < kernelSize[0]; s++) {
                        for (int t = 0; t < kernelSize[1]; t++) {
                            convolved_ += W[k][c][s][t] *
                            x[c][i+s][j+t];
                        }
                    }
                }

                // cache pre-activated inputs
                preActivated_X[k][i][j] = convolved_ + b[k];
                activated_X[k][i][j] =
                this.activation.apply(preActivated_X[k][i][j]);
                y[k][i][j] = activated_X[k][i][j];
            }
        }
    }

    return y;
}
```

The `downsample` method follows the equations as well:

```java
public double[][][] downsample(double[][][] x) {

    double[][][] y = new double[nKernel][pooledSize[0]][pooledSize[1]];

    for (int k = 0; k < nKernel; k++) {
        for (int i = 0; i < pooledSize[0]; i++) {
```

```
                    for (int j = 0; j < pooledSize[1]; j++) {

                        double max_ = 0.;

                        for (int s = 0; s < poolSize[0]; s++) {
                            for (int t = 0; t < poolSize[1]; t++) {

                                if (s == 0 && t == 0) {
                                    max_ =
                                    x[k][poolSize[0]*i][poolSize[1]*j];
                                    continue;
                                }
                                if (max_ <
                                x[k][poolSize[0]*i+s][poolSize[1]*j+t]) {
                                    max_ =
                                    x[k][poolSize[0]*i+s][poolSize[1]*j+t];
                                }
                            }
                        }

                        y[k][i][j] = max_;
                    }
                }
            }

        return y;
    }
```

You might think we've made some mistake here because there are so many `for` loops in these methods, but actually there's nothing wrong. As you can see from the equations of CNN, the algorithm requires many loops because it has many parameters. The code here works well, but practically, you could define and move the part of the innermost loops to other methods. Here, to get a better understanding, we've implemented CNN with many nested loops so that we can compare the code with equations. You can see now that CNN requires a lot of time to get results.

After we downsample the data, we need to flatten it:

```
// flatten output to make it input for fully connected MLP
double[] x_ = this.flatten(z_);
flattened_X[n] = x_.clone();
```

The data is then forwarded to the hidden layer:

```
// forward hidden layer
Z[n] = hiddenLayer.forward(x_);
```

Multi-class logistic regression is used in the output layer and the delta is then backpropagated to the hidden layer:

```
// forward & backward output layer
dY = logisticLayer.train(Z, T, minibatchSize, learningRate);

// backward hidden layer
dZ = hiddenLayer.backward(flattened_X, Z, dY, logisticLayer.W,
minibatchSize, learningRate);

// backpropagate delta to input layer
for (int n = 0; n < minibatchSize; n++) {
    for (int i = 0; i < flattenedSize; i++) {
        for (int j = 0; j < nHidden; j++) {
            dX_flatten[n][i] += hiddenLayer.W[j][i] * dZ[n][j];
        }
    }

    dX[n] = unflatten(dX_flatten[n]);  // unflatten delta
}

// backward convolution + pooling layers
dC = dX.clone();
for (int i = nKernels.length-1; i >= 0; i--) {
    dC = convpoolLayers[i].backward(downsampled_X.get(i),
    preActivated_X.get(i), activated_X.get(i),
    downsampled_X.get(i+1), dC, minibatchSize, learningRate);
}
```

The `backward` method of `ConvolutionPoolingLayer` is the same as `forward`, also simple. Backpropagation of max-pooling is written in `upsample` and that of convolution is in `deconvolve`:

```
public double[][][][] backward(double[][][][] X, double[][][]
[] preActivated_X, double[][][][] activated_X, double[][][]
[] downsampled_X, double[][][][] dY, int minibatchSize, double
learningRate) {

    double[][][][] dZ = this.upsample(activated_X, downsampled_X,
    dY, minibatchSize);
    return this.deconvolve(X, preActivated_X, dZ, minibatchSize,
    learningRate);

}
```

What `upsample` does is just transfer the delta to the convolutional layer:

```
public double[][][][] upsample(double[][][][] X, double[][][][] Y,
double[][][][] dY, int minibatchSize) {

    double[][][][] dX = new double[minibatchSize][nKernel]
[convolvedSize[0]][convolvedSize[1]];

    for (int n = 0; n < minibatchSize; n++) {

        for (int k = 0; k < nKernel; k++) {
            for (int i = 0; i < pooledSize[0]; i++) {
                for (int j = 0; j < pooledSize[1]; j++) {

                    for (int s = 0; s < poolSize[0]; s++) {
                        for (int t = 0; t < poolSize[1]; t++) {

                            double d_ = 0.;

                            if (Y[n][k][i][j] == X[n][k]
[poolSize[0]*i+s][poolSize[1]*j+t]) {
                                d_ = dY[n][k][i][j];
                            }

                            dX[n][k][poolSize[0]*i+s][poolSize[1]*j+t]
= d_;
                        }
                    }
                }
            }
        }
    }

    return dX;
}
```

In `deconvolve`, we need to update the model parameter. Since we train the model with mini-batches, we calculate the summation of the gradients first:

```
// calc gradients of W, b
for (int n = 0; n < minibatchSize; n++) {
    for (int k = 0; k < nKernel; k++) {

        for (int i = 0; i < convolvedSize[0]; i++) {
```

```
            for (int j = 0; j < convolvedSize[1]; j++) {

                double d_ = dY[n][k][i][j] *
                this.dactivation.apply(Y[n][k][i][j]);

                grad_b[k] += d_;

                for (int c = 0; c < channel; c++) {
                    for (int s = 0; s < kernelSize[0]; s++) {
                        for (int t = 0; t < kernelSize[1]; t++) {
                            grad_W[k][c][s][t] += d_ *
                            X[n][c][i+s][j+t];
                        }
                    }
                }
            }
        }
    }
}
```

Then, update the weight and the bias using these gradients:

```
// update gradients
for (int k = 0; k < nKernel; k++) {
    b[k] -= learningRate * grad_b[k] / minibatchSize;

    for (int c = 0; c < channel; c++) {
        for (int s = 0; s < kernelSize[0]; s++) {
            for(int t = 0; t < kernelSize[1]; t++) {
                W[k][c][s][t] -= learningRate * grad_W[k][c][s][t] /
minibatchSize;
            }
        }
    }
}
```

Unlike other algorithms, we have to calculate the parameters and delta discretely in CNN:

```
// calc delta
for (int n = 0; n < minibatchSize; n++) {
    for (int c = 0; c < channel; c++) {
        for (int i = 0; i < imageSize[0]; i++) {
            for (int j = 0; j < imageSize[1]; j++) {

                for (int k = 0; k < nKernel; k++) {
```

```
            for (int s = 0; s < kernelSize[0]; s++) {
                for (int t = 0; t < kernelSize[1]; t++) {

                    double d_ = 0.;

                    if (i - (kernelSize[0] - 1) - s >= 0 &&
                     j - (kernelSize[1] - 1) - t >= 0) {
                        d_ = dY[n][k][i-(kernelSize[0]-1)-
                        s][j-(kernelSize[1]-1)-t] *
                        this.dactivation.apply(Y[n][k]
                        [i- (kernelSize[0]-1)-s]
                        [j-(kernelSize[1]-1)-t]) *
                        W[k][c][s][t];
                    }

                    dX[n][c][i][j] += d_;
                }
            }
        }
    }
}
```

Now we train the model, so let's go on to the test part. The method for testing or prediction simply does the forward propagation, just like the other algorithms:

```
public Integer[] predict(double[][][] x) {

    List<double[][][]> preActivated = new ArrayList<>(nKernels.length);
    List<double[][][]> activated = new ArrayList<>(nKernels.length);

    for (int i = 0; i < nKernels.length; i++) {
        preActivated.add(new
        double[nKernels[i]][convolvedSizes[i][0]]
        [convolvedSizes[i][1]]);
        activated.add(new double[nKernels[i]][convolvedSizes[i][0]]
        [convolvedSizes[i][1]]);
    }

    // forward convolution + pooling layers
    double[][][] z = x.clone();
    for (int i = 0; i < nKernels.length; i++) {
```

```
        z = convpoolLayers[i].forward(z, preActivated.get(i),
        activated.get(i));
    }


    // forward MLP
    return logisticLayer.predict(hiddenLayer.forward(this.flatten(z)));
}
```

Congratulations! That's all for CNN. Now you can run the code and see how it works. Here, we have CNN with two-dimensional data as input, but CNN can also have three-dimensional data if we expand the model. We can expect its application in medical fields, for example, finding malignant tumors from 3D-scanned data of human brains.

The process of convolution and pooling was originally invented by LeCun et al. in 1998 (`http://yann.lecun.com/exdb/publis/pdf/lecun-98.pdf`), yet as you can see from the codes, it requires much calculation. We can assume that this method might not have been suitable for practical applications with computers at the time, not to mention making it deep. The reason CNN has gained more attention recently is probably because the power and capacity of computers has greatly developed. But still, we can't deny the problem. Therefore, it seems practical to use GPU, not CPU, when we have CNN with certain amounts of data. Since the implementation to optimize the algorithm to GPU is complicated, we won't write the codes here. Instead, in *Chapter 5*, *Exploring Java Deep Learning Libraries – DL4J, ND4J, and More* and *Chapter 7*, *Other Important Deep Learning Libraries*, you'll see the library of deep learning that is capable of utilizing GPU.

Summary

In this chapter, you learned about two deep learning algorithms that don't require pre-training: deep neural networks with dropout and CNN. The key to high precision rates is how we make the network sparse, and dropout is one technique to achieve this. Another technique is the rectifier, the activation function that can solve the problem of saturation that occurred in the sigmoid function and the hyperbolic tangent. CNN is the most popular algorithm for image recognition and has two features: convolution and max-pooling. Both of these attribute the model to acquire translation invariance. If you are interested in how dropout, rectifier, and other activation functions contribute to the performance of neural networks, the following could be good references: *Deep Sparse Rectifier Neural Networks* (Glorot, et. al. 2011, `http://www.jmlr.org/proceedings/papers/v15/glorot11a/glorot11a.pdf`), *ImageNet Classification with Deep Convolutional Neural Networks* (Krizhevsky et. al. 2012, `https://papers.nips.cc/paper/4824-imagenet-classification-with-deep-convolutional-neural-networks.pdf`), and *Maxout Networks* (Goodfellow et al. 2013, `http://arxiv.org/pdf/1302.4389.pdf`).

While you now know the popular and useful deep learning algorithms, there are still many of them that have not been mentioned in this book. This field of study is getting more and more active, and more and more new algorithms are appearing. But don't worry, as all the algorithms are based on the same root: neural networks. Now you know the way of thinking required to grasp or implement the model, you can fully understand whatever models you encounter.

We've implemented deep learning algorithms from scratch so you fully understand them. In the next chapter, you'll see how we can implement them with deep learning libraries to facilitate our research or applications.

5
Exploring Java Deep Learning Libraries -- DL4J, ND4J, and More

In the previous chapters, you learned the core theories of deep learning algorithms and implemented them from scratch. While we can now say that implementations of deep learning are not so difficult, we can't deny the fact that it still takes some time to implement models. To mitigate this situation, you'll learn how to write code with the Java library of deep learning in this chapter so that we can focus more on the critical part of data analysis rather than the trivial part.

The topics you'll learn about in this chapter are:

- An introduction to the deep learning library of Java
- Example code and how to write your own code with the library
- Some additional ways to optimize the model to get a higher precision rate

Implementing from scratch versus a library/framework

We implemented the machine learning algorithms of neural networks in *Chapter 2, Algorithms for Machine Learning – Preparing for Deep Learning,* and many deep learning algorithms from scratch in *Chapter 3, Deep Belief Nets and Stacked Denoising Autoencoders* and *Chapter 4, Dropout and Convolutional Neural Networks*. Of course, we can apply our own code to practical applications with some customizations, but we have to be careful when we want to utilize them because we can't deny the possibility that they might cause several problems in the future. What could they be? Here are the possible situations:

- The code we wrote has some missing parameters for better optimization because we implemented just the essence of the algorithms for simplicity and so you better understand the concepts. While you can still train and optimize the model with them, you could get higher precision rates by adding another parameter of your own implementation.

- As mentioned in the previous chapter, there are still many useful deep learning algorithms not explained in this book. While you now have the core components of the deep learning algorithms, you might need to implement additional classes or methods to get the desired results in your fields and applications.

- The assumed time consumption will be very critical to the application, especially when you think of analyzing huge amounts of data. It is true that Java has a better performance in terms of speed compared to other popular languages such as Python and R, but you may still need to consider the time cost. One plausible approach to solve the problem is using GPU instead of CPU, but this requires complex implementations to adjust the code for GPU computing.

These are the main causal issues, and you might also need to take into consideration that we don't handle exceptions in the code.

This does not mean that implementing from scratch would have fatal errors. The code we wrote can be used substantially as an application for certain scaled data; however, you need to take into consideration that you require further coding for the fundamental parts you have implemented if you use large-scale data mining, where, generally, deep learning is required. This means you need to bear in mind that implementation from scratch has more flexibility as you can change the code if required, but at the same time it has a negative side in that the algorithm's tuning and maintenance also has to be done independently.

So, how can we solve the problems just mentioned? This is where a library (or framework) comes in. Thanks to active research into deep learning globally, there are many libraries developed and published using various programming languages all over the world. Of course, each library has its respective features but the features that every library commonly has can be summarized as follows:

- A model's training can be done just by defining a layer structure of deep learning. You can focus on parameter setting and tuning, and you don't need to think about the algorithms.

- Most of the libraries are open to the public as open source projects and are actively updated daily. Therefore, if there are bugs, there's a high possibility that these bugs will be fixed quickly (and, of course, committing to a project by fixing it yourself should be welcomed).

- It's easy to switch between running the program on CPU or on GPU. As a library supplements the cumbersome coding element of GPU computing, you can just focus on the implementation without considering CPU or GPU, if a machine supports GPU.

Long story short, you can leave out all the parts that could be brutal when you implement to a library from scratch. Thanks to this, you can take more time on the essential data mining section, hence if you want to utilize practical applications, there's a high possibility that you can perform data analysis more efficiently using a library.

However, depending too much on a library isn't good. Using a library is convenient, but on the flip side, it has some demerits, as listed here:

- Since you can build various deep learning models easily, you can implement without having a concrete understanding of what theory the model is supported by. This might not be a problem if we only consider implementations related to a specific model, but there will be a risk you can't deal with when you want to combine other methods or consider other methods when applying the model.

- You can't use algorithms not supported by a library, hence there might be a case where you can't choose a model you would like to use. This can be solved by a version upgrade, but on the other hand, there's a possibility that some part of a past implementation might be deprecated due to a change of specification by the upgrade. Moreover, we can't deny the possibility that the development of a library is suddenly terminated or utilization turns out to be chargeable due to a sudden change in its license. In these cases, there's a risk that the code you have developed up to this point cannot be used.

- The precision rate you can get from experimentation depends on how a library is implemented. For example, if we conduct an experiment with the same neural network model in two different libraries, the results we obtain can be hugely changed. This is because neural network algorithms include a stochastic operation, and the calculation accuracy of a machine is limited, that is, calculated values during the process could have fluctuations based on the method of implementation.

Because you well understand the fundamental concepts and theories of deep learning algorithms thanks to the previous chapters, we don't need to worry about the first point. However, we need to be careful about the remaining two points. From the next section on, implementation using a library is introduced and we'll be more conscious of the merits and demerits we just discussed.

Introducing DL4J and ND4J

A lot of the libraries of deep learning have been developed all over the world. In November 2015, **TensorFlow** (http://www.tensorflow.org/), a machine learning/deep learning library developed by Google, became open to the public and attracted great attention.

When we look at the programming language with which libraries are being developed, most of them open to the public are developed by Python or use the Python API. TensorFlow is developed with C++ on the backend but it's also possible to write code with Python. This book focuses on Java to learn deep learning, hence the libraries developed by other languages will be briefly introduced in *Chapter 7, Other Important Deep Learning Libraries*.

So, what Java-based libraries do we have? Actually, there are a few cases that are actively developed (perhaps there are also some projects not open to public). However, there is only one library we can use practically: **Deeplearning4j (DL4J)**. The official project page URL is http://deeplearning4j.org/. This library is also open source and the source code is all published on GitHub. The URL is https://github.com/deeplearning4j/deeplearning4j. This library was developed by Skymind (http://www.skymind.io/). What kind of library is this? If you look at the project page, it's introduced as follows:

> *"Deeplearning4j is the first commercial-grade, open-source, distributed deep-learning library written for Java and Scala. Integrated with Hadoop and Spark, DL4J is designed to be used in business environments, rather than as a research tool. Skymind is its commercial support arm.*

Deeplearning4j aims to be cutting-edge plug and play, more convention than configuration, which allows for fast prototyping for non-researchers. DL4J is customizable at scale. Released under the Apache 2.0 license, all derivatives of DL4J belong to their authors."

When you read this, you will see that the biggest feature of DL4J is that it was designed on the premise of being integrated with Hadoop. This indicates that DL4J suits the processing of large-scale data and is more scalable than other libraries. Moreover, DL4J supports GPU computing, so it's possible to process data even faster.

Also, DL4J uses a library called **N-Dimensional Arrays for Java (ND4J)** internally. The project page is `http://nd4j.org/`. The same as DL4J, this library is also published on GitHub as an open source project: `https://github.com/deeplearning4j/nd4j`. The developer of the library is the same as DL4J, Skymind. As you can see from the name of the library, this is a scientific computing library that enables us to handle versatile *n*-dimensional array objects. If you are a Python developer, it might be easier for you to understand this if you imagine NumPy, as ND4J is a library inspired by NumPy. ND4J also supports GPU computing and the reason why DL4J is able to do GPU integration is because it uses ND4J internally.

What good can come from working with them on GPUs? Let's briefly look at this point. The biggest difference between CPU and GPU is the difference in the number of cores. GPU is, as represented in its name, a graphical processing unit, originally an integrated circuit for image processing. This is why GPU is well optimized to handle the same commands simultaneously. Parallel processing is its forte. On the other hand, as CPU needs to process various commands, these tasks are basically made to be processed in order. Compared to CPU, GPU is good at processing huge numbers of simple tasks, therefore calculations such as training iterations of deep learning is its field of expertise.

Both ND4J and DL4J are very useful for research and data mining with deep learning. From the next section on, we'll see how these are used for deep learning in simple examples. You can easily understand the contents because you should already understand the core theories of deep learning by now. Hopefully, you can make use of this for your fields of study or business.

Implementations with ND4J

As there are many cases where ND4J alone can be used conveniently, let's briefly grasp how to use ND4J before looking into the explanation of DL4J. If you would like to use ND4J alone, once you create a new Maven project, then you can use ND4J by adding the following code to pom.xml:

```
<properties>
    <nd4j.version>0.4-rc3.6</nd4j.version>
</properties>

<dependencies>
    <dependency>
        <groupId>org.nd4j</groupId>
        <artifactId>nd4j-jblas</artifactId>
        <version>${nd4j.version}</version>
    </dependency>
    <dependency>
        <groupId>org.nd4j</groupId>
        <artifactId>nd4j-perf</artifactId>
        <version>${nd4j.version}</version>
    </dependency>
</dependencies>
```

Here, `<nd4j.version>` describes the latest version of ND4J, but please check whether it is updated when you actually implement the code. Also, switching from CPU to GPU is easy while working with ND4J. If you have CUDA installed with version 7.0, then what you do is just define `artifactId` as follows:

```
<dependency>
    <groupId>org.nd4j</groupId>
    <artifactId>nd4j-jcublas-7.0</artifactId>
    <version>${nd4j.version}</version>
</dependency>
```

You can replace the version of `<artifactId>` depending on your configuration.

Let's look at a simple example of what calculations are possible with ND4J. The type we utilize with ND4J is `INDArray`, that is, an extended type of `Array`. We begin by importing the following dependencies:

```
import org.nd4j.linalg.api.ndarray.INDArray;
import org.nd4j.linalg.factory.Nd4j;
```

Then, we define INDArray as follows:

```
INDArray x = Nd4j.create(new double[]{1, 2, 3, 4, 5, 6}, new
int[]{3, 2});
System.out.println(x);
```

Nd4j.create takes two arguments. The former defines the actual values within INDArray, and the latter defines the shape of the vector (matrix). By running this code, you get the following result:

```
[[1.00,2.00]
 [3.00,4.00]
 [5.00,6.00]]
```

Since INDArray can output its values with System.out.print, it's easy to debug. Calculation with scalar can also be done with ease. Add 1 to x as shown here:

```
x.add(1);
```

Then, you will get the following output:

```
[[2.00,3.00]
 [4.00,5.00]
 [6.00,7.00]]
```

Also, the calculation within INDArray can be done easily, as shown in the following example:

```
INDArray y = Nd4j.create(new double[]{6, 5, 4, 3, 2, 1}, new
int[]{3, 2});
```

Then, basic arithmetic operations can be represented as follows:

```
x.add(y)
x.sub(y)
x.mul(y)
x.div(y)
```

These will return the following result:

```
[[7.00,7.00]
 [7.00,7.00]
 [7.00,7.00]]
[[-5.00,-3.00]
 [-1.00,1.00]
 [3.00,5.00]]
[[6.00,10.00]
```

```
   [12.00,12.00]
   [10.00,6.00]]
 [[0.17,0.40]
  [0.75,1.33]
  [2.50,6.00]]
```

Also, ND4J has destructive arithmetic operators. When you write the `x.addi(y)` command, x changes its own values so that `System.out.println(x);` will return the following output:

```
[[7.00,7.00]
 [7.00,7.00]
 [7.00,7.00]]
```

Likewise, `subi`, `muli`, and `divi` are also destructive operators. There are also many other methods that can conveniently perform calculations between vectors or matrices. For more information, you can refer to `http://nd4j.org/documentation.html`, `http://nd4j.org/doc/` and `http://nd4j.org/apidocs/`.

Let's look at one more example to see how machine learning algorithms can be written with ND4J. We'll implement the easiest example, perceptrons, based on the source code written in *Chapter 2, Algorithms for Machine Learning – Preparing for Deep Learning*. We set the package name `DLWJ.examples.ND4J` and the file (class) name `Perceptrons.java`.

First, let's add these two lines to import from ND4J:

```
import org.nd4j.linalg.api.ndarray.INDArray;
import org.nd4j.linalg.factory.Nd4j;
```

The model has two parameters: `num` of the input layer and the weight. The former doesn't change from the previous code; however, the latter isn't `Array` but `INDArray`:

```
public int nIn;        // dimensions of input data
public INDArray w;
```

You can see from the constructor that since the weight of the perceptrons is represented as a vector, the number of rows is set to the number of units in the input layer and the number of columns to 1. This definition is written here:

```
public Perceptrons(int nIn) {

    this.nIn = nIn;
    w = Nd4j.create(new double[nIn], new int[]{nIn, 1});

}
```

Then, because we define the model parameter as INDArray, we also define the demo data, training data, and test data as INDArray. You can see these definitions at the beginning of the main method:

```
INDArray train_X = Nd4j.create(new double[train_N * nIn], new int[]
{train_N, nIn});  // input data for training
INDArray train_T = Nd4j.create(new double[train_N], new int[]{train_N,
1});           // output data (label) for training

INDArray test_X = Nd4j.create(new double[test_N * nIn], new int[]
{test_N, nIn});  // input data for test
INDArray test_T = Nd4j.create(new double[test_N], new int[]{test_N,
1});           // label of inputs
INDArray predicted_T = Nd4j.create(new double[test_N], new int[]
{test_N, 1});      // output data predicted by the model
```

When we substitute a value into INDArray, we use put. Please be careful that any value we can set with put is only the values of the scalar type:

```
train_X.put(i, 0, Nd4j.scalar(g1.random()));
train_X.put(i, 1, Nd4j.scalar(g2.random()));
train_T.put(i, Nd4j.scalar(1));
```

The flow from a model building and training is the same as the previous code:

```
// construct perceptrons
Perceptrons classifier = new Perceptrons(nIn);

// train models
while (true) {
    int classified_ = 0;

    for (int i=0; i < train_N; i++) {
        classified_ += classifier.train(train_X.getRow(i),
        train_T.getRow(i), learningRate);
    }

    if (classified_ == train_N) break;  // when all data classified
    correctly

    epoch++;
    if (epoch > epochs) break;
}
```

Each piece of training data is given to the `train` method by `getRow()`. First, let's see the entire content of the `train` method:

```
public int train(INDArray x, INDArray t, double learningRate) {

    int classified = 0;

    // check if the data is classified correctly
    double c = x.mmul(w).getDouble(0) * t.getDouble(0);

    // apply steepest descent method if the data is wrongly
    classified
    if (c > 0) {
        classified = 1;
    } else {
        w.addi(x.transpose().mul(t).mul(learningRate));
    }

    return classified;
}
```

We first focus our attention on the following code:

```
// check if the data is classified correctly
double c = x.mmul(w).getDouble(0) * t.getDouble(0);
```

This is the part that checks whether the data is classified correctly by perceptions, as shown in the following equation:

$$w^T x_n t_n > 0$$

You can see from the code that `.mmul()` is for the multiplication between vectors or matrices. We wrote this part of the calculation in *Chapter 2, Algorithms for Machine Learning – Preparing for Deep Learning*, as follows:

```
double c = 0.;

// check if the data is classified correctly
for (int i = 0; i < nIn; i++) {
    c += w[i] * x[i] * t;
}
```

By comparing both codes, you can see that multiplication between vectors or matrices can be written easily with `INDArray`, and so you can implement the algorithm intuitively just by following the equations.

The equation to update the model parameters is as follows:

```
w.addi(x.transpose().mul(t).mul(learningRate));
```

Here, again, you can implement the code like you write a math equation. The equation is represented as follows:

$$w^{(k+1)} = w^{(k)} + \eta x_n t_n$$

The last time we implemented this part, we wrote it with a `for` loop:

```
for (int i = 0; i < nIn; i++) {
    w[i] += learningRate * x[i] * t;
}
```

Furthermore, the prediction after the training is also the standard forward activation, shown as the following equation:

$$y(x) = f\left(w^T x\right)$$

Here:

$$f(a) = \begin{cases} +1, & a \geq 0 \\ -1, & a < 0 \end{cases}$$

We can simply define the `predict` method with just a single line inside, as follows:

```
public int predict(INDArray x) {

    return step(x.mmul(w).getDouble(0));
}
```

When you run the program, you can see its precision and accuracy, and the recall is the same as we get with the previous code.

Thus, it'll greatly help that you implement the algorithms analogous to mathematical equations. We only implement perceptrons here, but please try other algorithms by yourself.

Implementations with DL4J

ND4J is the library that helps you to implement deep learning easily and conveniently. However, you have to implement the algorithms yourself, which is not too different from its implementation in the previous chapters. In other words, ND4J is just a library that makes calculating numerical values easier and is not a library that is optimized for deep learning algorithms. One library that makes deep learning easier to handle is DL4J. Fortunately, as for DL4J, some example code with typical methods is published on GitHub (`https://github.com/deeplearning4j/dl4j-0.4-examples`). These examples are used on the premise that you are using DL4J's version 0.4-*. When you actually clone this repository, please check the latest version again. In this section, we'll extract the fundamental part from these sample programs and take a look at it. We'll reference the forked repository on `https://github.com/yusugomori/dl4j-0.4-examples` as a screenshot in this section.

Setup

Let's first set up the environments from our cloned repository. If you're using IntelliJ, you can import the project from **File | New | Project** from existing sources and select the path of the repository. Then, choose **Import project from external model** and select **Maven** as follows:

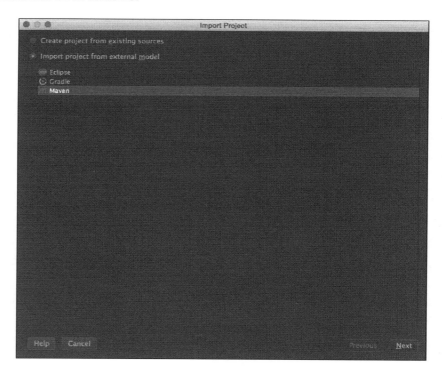

You don't have to do anything special for the other steps except click **Next**. Please be careful that the supported versions of JDK are 1.7 or above. This may not be a problem because we needed version 1.8 or above in the previous chapters. Once you have set it up without a problem, you can confirm the structure of the directories as follows:

Once you have set up the project, let's first look at pom.xml. You can see that the description of the packages related to DL4J is written as:

```xml
<dependency>
    <groupId>org.deeplearning4j</groupId>
    <artifactId>deeplearning4j-nlp</artifactId>
    <version>${dl4j.version}</version>
</dependency>

<dependency>
    <groupId>org.deeplearning4j</groupId>
    <artifactId>deeplearning4j-core</artifactId>
    <version>${dl4j.version}</version>
</dependency>
```

Also, you can see from the following lines that DL4J depends on ND4J:

```
<dependency>
    <groupId>org.nd4j</groupId>
    <artifactId>nd4j-x86</artifactId>
    <version>${nd4j.version}</version>
</dependency>
```

If you would like to run a program on GPU, what you have to do is just change this written section. As mentioned in the previous section, this can be written as follows if you have CUDA installed:

```
<dependency>
    <groupId>org.nd4j</groupId>
    <artifactId>nd4j-jcublas-XXX</artifactId>
    <version>${nd4j.version}</version>
</dependency>
```

Here, XXX is the version of CUDA and depends on your machine's preference. It's great to adopt GPU computing only using this. We don't have to do anything special and we can focus on implementations of deep learning.

The other characteristic library that DL4J develops and uses is **Canova**. The part that corresponds to pom.xml is as follows:

```
<dependency>
    <artifactId>canova-nd4j-image</artifactId>
    <groupId>org.nd4j</groupId>
    <version>${canova.version}</version>
</dependency>
<dependency>
    <artifactId>canova-nd4j-codec</artifactId>
    <groupId>org.nd4j</groupId>
    <version>${canova.version}</version>
</dependency>
```

Canova is also, of course, an open source library and its source code can be seen on GitHub at https://github.com/deeplearning4j/Canova. As explained on that page, Canova is the library used to vectorize raw data into usable vector formats across the machine learning tools. This also helps us focus on the more important part of data mining because data formatting is indispensable in whatever research or experiment we're performing.

Build

Let's look at the source code in the examples and see how to build a deep learning model. During the process, the terms of deep learning that you haven't yet learned are also briefly explained. The examples are implemented with various models such as MLP, DBN, and CNN, but there is one problem here. As you can see when looking at README.md, some methods don't generate good precision. This is because, as explained in the previous section, the calculation precision a machine has is limited and fluctuation occurring with calculated values during the process depends completely on the difference of implementation. Hence, practically, learning can't be done properly, although theoretically it should be done well. You can get better results by, for example, changing the seed values or adjusting the parameters, but as we would like to focus on how to use a library, we'll use a model that gets higher precision as an example.

DBNIrisExample.java

Let's first look at DBNIrisExample.java in the package of deepbelief. Iris, contained in the filename, is one of the benchmark datasets often used when measuring the precision or accuracy of a machine learning method. The dataset contains 150 pieces of data out of 3 classes of 50 instances each, and each class refers to a type of Iris plant. The number of inputs is 4 and the number of outputs is therefore 3. One class is linearly separable from the other two; the latter are not linearly separable from each other.

The implementation begins by setting up the configuration. Here are the variables that need setting:

```
final int numRows = 4;
final int numColumns = 1;
int outputNum = 3;
int numSamples = 150;
int batchSize = 150;
int iterations = 5;
int splitTrainNum = (int) (batchSize * .8);
int seed = 123;
int listenerFreq = 1;
```

In DL4J, input data can be up to two-dimensional data, hence you need to assign the number of rows and columns of the data. As Iris is one-dimensional data, `numColumns` is set as 1. Here `numSamples` is the total data and `batchSize` is the amount of data in each mini-batch. Since the total data is 150 and it is relatively small, `batchSize` is set at the same number. This means that learning is done without splitting the data into mini-batches. `splitTrainNum` is the variable that decides the allocation between the training data and test data. Here, 80% of all the dataset is training data and 20% is the test data. In the previous section, `listenerFreq` decides how often we see loss function's value for logging is seen in the process. This value is set to 1 here, which means the value is logged after each epoch.

Subsequently, we need to fetch the dataset. In DL4J, a class that can easily fetch data with respect to a typical dataset, such as Iris, MINST, and LFW, is prepared. Therefore, you can just write the following line if you would like to fetch the Iris dataset:

```
DataSetIterator iter = new IrisDataSetIterator(batchSize, numSamples);
```

The following two lines are to format data:

```
DataSet next = iter.next();
next.normalizeZeroMeanZeroUnitVariance();
```

This code splits the data into training data and test data and stores them respectively:

```
SplitTestAndTrain testAndTrain =
next.splitTestAndTrain(splitTrainNum, new Random(seed));
DataSet train = testAndTrain.getTrain();
DataSet test = testAndTrain.getTest();
```

As you can see, it makes data handling easier by treating all the data DL4J prepares with the `DataSet` class.

Now, let's actually build a model. The basic structure is as follows:

```
MultiLayerConfiguration conf = new
NeuralNetConfiguration.Builder().layer().layer() … .layer().build();
MultiLayerNetwork model = new MultiLayerNetwork(conf);
model.init();
```

The code begins by defining the model configuration and then builds and initializes the actual model with the definition. Let's take a look at the configuration details. At the beginning, the whole network is set up:

```
MultiLayerConfiguration conf = new NeuralNetConfiguration.Builder()
    .seed(seed)
    .iterations(iterations)
```

```
.learningRate(1e-6f)
.optimizationAlgo(OptimizationAlgorithm.CONJUGATE_GRADIENT)
.l1(1e-1).regularization(true).l2(2e-4)
.useDropConnect(true)
.list(2)
```

The configuration setup is self-explanatory. However, since you haven't learned about regularization before now, let's briefly check it out.

Regularization prevents the neural networks model from overfitting and makes the model more generalized. To achieve this, the evaluation function $E(w)$ is rewritten with the penalty term as follows:

$$E(w) + \lambda \frac{1}{p} \|w\|_p^p = E(w) + \lambda \frac{1}{p} \sum_i |w_i|^p$$

Here, $\|\cdot\|$ denotes the vector norm. The regularization is called L1 regularization when $p = 1$ and L2 regularization when $p = 2$. The norm is called L1 norm and L2 norm, respectively. That's why we have .l1() and .l2() in the code. λ is the hyper parameter. These regularization terms make the model more sparse. L2 regularization is also called weight decay and is used to prevent the vanishing gradient problem.

The .useDropConnect() command is used to enable dropout and .list() to define the number of layers, excluding the input layer.

When you set up a whole model, then the next step is to configure each layer. In this sample code, the model is not defined as deep neural networks. One single RBM layer is defined as a hidden layer:

```
.layer(0, new RBM.Builder(RBM.HiddenUnit.RECTIFIED, RBM.VisibleUnit.
GAUSSIAN)
 .nIn(numRows * numColumns)
 .nOut(3)
 .weightInit(WeightInit.XAVIER)
 .k(1)
 .activation("relu")
 .lossFunction(LossFunctions.LossFunction.RMSE_XENT)
 .updater(Updater.ADAGRAD)
 .dropOut(0.5)
 .build()
)
```

Here, the value of 0 in the first line is the layer's index and .k() is for contrastive divergence. Since Iris' data is of float values, we can't use binary RBM. That's why we have RBM.VisibleUnit.GAUSSIAN here, enabling the model to handle continuous values. Also, as for the definition of this layer, what should be especially mentioned is the role of Updater.ADAGRAD. This is used to optimize the learning rate. For now, we go on to the model structure, and a detailed explanation of the optimizer will be introduced at the end of this chapter.

The subsequent output layer is very simple and self-explanatory:

```
.layer(1, new OutputLayer.Builder(LossFunctions.LossFunction.MCXENT)
  .nIn(3)
  .nOut(outputNum)
  .activation("softmax")
  .build()
)
```

Thus, the neural networks have been built with three layers : input layer, hidden layer, and output layer. The graphical model of this example can be illustrated as follows:

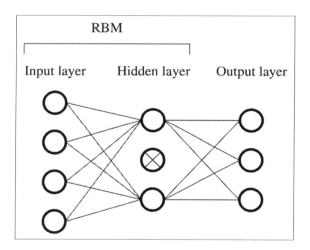

After the model building, we need to train the networks. Here, again, the code is super simple:

```
model.setListeners(Arrays.asList((IterationListener) new
ScoreIterationListener(listenerFreq)));
model.fit(train);
```

Because the first line is to log the process, what we need to do to train the model is just to write model.fit().

Testing or evaluating the model is also easy with DL4J. First, the variables for evaluation are set up as follows:

```
Evaluation eval = new Evaluation(outputNum);
INDArray output = model.output(test.getFeatureMatrix());
```

Then, we can get the values of the feature matrix using:

```
eval.eval(test.getLabels(), output);
log.info(eval.stats());
```

By running the code, we will have the result as follows:

```
=========================Scores=========================================
 Accuracy:   0.7667
 Precision:  1
 Recall:     0.7667
 F1 Score:   0.8679245283018869

========================================================================
```

`F1 Score`, also called `F-Score` or `F-measure`, is the harmonic means of precision and recall, and is represented as follows:

$$F_1 = 2.\frac{Precision.Recall}{Precision+Recall}$$

This value is often calculated to measure the model's performance as well. Also, as written in the example, you can see the actual values and predicted values by writing the following:

```
for (int i = 0; i < output.rows(); i++) {
    String actual = test.getLabels().getRow(i).toString().trim();
    String predicted = output.getRow(i).toString().trim();
    log.info("actual " + actual + " vs predicted " + predicted);
}
```

That's it for the whole training and test process. The neural networks in the preceding code are not deep, but you can easily build deep neural networks just by changing the configuration as follows:

```
MultiLayerConfiguration conf = new NeuralNetConfiguration.Builder()
        .seed(seed)
        .iterations(iterations)
        .learningRate(1e-6f)
```

```
            .optimizationAlgo(OptimizationAlgorithm.CONJUGATE_GRADIENT)
            .l1(1e-1).regularization(true).l2(2e-4)
            .useDropConnect(true)
            .list(3)
            .layer(0, new RBM.Builder(RBM.HiddenUnit.RECTIFIED, RBM.
VisibleUnit.GAUSSIAN)
                        .nIn(numRows * numColumns)
                        .nOut(4)
                        .weightInit(WeightInit.XAVIER)
                        .k(1)
                        .activation("relu")
                        .lossFunction(LossFunctions.LossFunction.RMSE_
XENT)
                        .updater(Updater.ADAGRAD)
                        .dropOut(0.5)
                        .build()
            )
            .layer(1, new RBM.Builder(RBM.HiddenUnit.RECTIFIED, RBM.
VisibleUnit.GAUSSIAN)
                        .nIn(4)
                        .nOut(3)
                        .weightInit(WeightInit.XAVIER)
                        .k(1)
                        .activation("relu")
                        .lossFunction(LossFunctions.LossFunction.RMSE_
XENT)
                        .updater(Updater.ADAGRAD)
                        .dropOut(0.5)
                        .build()
            )
            .layer(2, new OutputLayer.Builder(LossFunctions.LossFunction.
MCXENT)
                        .nIn(3)
                        .nOut(outputNum)
                        .activation("softmax")
                        .build()
            )
            .build();
```

As you can see, building deep neural networks requires just simple implementations with DL4J. Once you set up the model, what you need to do is adjust the parameters. For example, increasing the iterations value or changing the seed value would return a better result.

CSVExample.java

In the previous example, we train the model with the dataset used as a benchmark indicator. When you would like to train and test the model with your own prepared data, you can easily import it from CSV. Let's look at CSVExample.java in the CSV package. The first step is to initialize the CSV reader as follows:

```
RecordReader recordReader = new CSVRecordReader(0,",");
```

In DL4J, a class called CSVRecordReader is prepared and you can easily import data from a CSV file. The value of the first argument in the CSVRecordReader class represents how many lines should be skipped in the file. This is convenient when the file contains header rows. The second argument is the delimiter. To actually read a file and import data, the code can be written as follows:

```
recordReader.initialize(new FileSplit(new
ClassPathResource("iris.txt").getFile()));
```

With this code, the file in resources/iris.txt will be imported to the model. The values in the file here are the same as ones as in the Iris dataset. To use this initialized data for model training, we define the iterator as follows:

```
DataSetIterator iterator = new RecordReaderDataSetIterator(recordRead
er,4,3);
DataSet next = iterator.next();
```

In the previous example, we used the IrisDataSetIterator class, but here the RecordReaderDataSetIterator class is used because we use our own prepared data. The values 4 and 3 are the number of features and labels, respectively.

Building and training a model can be done in almost the same way as the process explained in the previous example. In this example, we build deep neural networks of two hidden layers with the dropout and the rectifier, that is, we have an input layer - hidden layer - hidden layer - output layer, as follows:

```
MultiLayerConfiguration conf = new NeuralNetConfiguration.Builder()
        .seed(seed)
        .iterations(iterations)
        .constrainGradientToUnitNorm(true).useDropConnect(true)
        .learningRate(1e-1)
        .l1(0.3).regularization(true).l2(1e-3)
        .constrainGradientToUnitNorm(true)
        .list(3)
        .layer(0, new DenseLayer.Builder().nIn(numInputs).nOut(3)
                .activation("relu").dropOut(0.5)
                .weightInit(WeightInit.XAVIER)
                .build())
```

```
        .layer(1, new DenseLayer.Builder().nIn(3).nOut(2)
                .activation("relu")
                .weightInit(WeightInit.XAVIER)
                .build())
        .layer(2, new
        OutputLayer.Builder(LossFunctions.LossFunction
        .NEGATIVELOGLIKELIHOOD)
                .weightInit(WeightInit.XAVIER)
                .activation("softmax")
                .nIn(2).nOut(outputNum).build())
        .backprop(true).pretrain(false)
        .build();
```

We can run the model using the following lines of code:

```
MultiLayerNetwork model = new MultiLayerNetwork(conf);
model.init();
```

The graphical model is as follows:

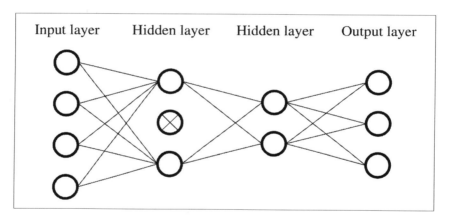

This time, however, the way to code for training is slightly different from the previous example. Before, we split the data into training data and test data using the following:

```
SplitTestAndTrain testAndTrain =
next.splitTestAndTrain(splitTrainNum, new Random(seed));
```

This shows that we shuffle the data within the .splitTestAndTrain() method. In this example, we set up training data with the following code:

```
next.shuffle();
SplitTestAndTrain testAndTrain = next.splitTestAndTrain(0.6);
```

As you can see, here the data is first shuffled and then split into training data and test data. Be careful that the types of the arguments in `.splitTestAndTrain()` are different from each other. This will be beneficial because we don't have to count the exact amount of data or training data. The actual training is done using:

```
model.fit(testAndTrain.getTrain());
```

The way to evaluate the model is just the same as the previous example:

```
Evaluation eval = new Evaluation(3);
DataSet test = testAndTrain.getTest();
INDArray output = model.output(test.getFeatureMatrix());
eval.eval(test.getLabels(), output);
log.info(eval.stats());
```

With the preceding code, we get the following result:

```
==========================Scores=====================================
Accuracy:    1
Precision: 1
Recall:      1
F1 Score:    1.0

=====================================================================
```

In addition to the dataset of a benchmark indicator, you can now analyze whatever data you have.

To make the model even deeper, you just need to add another layer as follows:

```
MultiLayerConfiguration conf = new
NeuralNetConfiguration.Builder()
        .seed(seed)
        .iterations(iterations)
        .constrainGradientToUnitNorm(true).useDropConnect(true)
        .learningRate(0.01)
        .l1(0.0).regularization(true).l2(1e-3)
        .constrainGradientToUnitNorm(true)
        .list(4)
        .layer(0, new DenseLayer.Builder().nIn(numInputs).nOut(4)
                .activation("relu").dropOut(0.5)
                .weightInit(WeightInit.XAVIER)
                .build())
        .layer(1, new DenseLayer.Builder().nIn(4).nOut(4)
                .activation("relu").dropOut(0.5)
                .weightInit(WeightInit.XAVIER)
```

```
        .build())
.layer(2, new DenseLayer.Builder().nIn(4).nOut(4)
        .activation("relu").dropOut(0.5)
        .weightInit(WeightInit.XAVIER)
        .build())
.layer(3, new
OutputLayer.Builder(LossFunctions.LossFunction
.NEGATIVELOGLIKELIHOOD)
        .weightInit(WeightInit.XAVIER)
        .activation("softmax")
        .nIn(4).nOut(outputNum).build())
.backprop(true).pretrain(false)
.build();
```

CNNMnistExample.java/LenetMnistExample.java

CNN is rather complicated compared to other models because of its structure, but we don't need to worry about these complications because we can easily implement CNN with DL4J. Let's take a look at CNNMnistExample.java in the package of convolution. In this example, we train the model with the MNIST dataset (http://yann.lecun. com/exdb/mnist/), one of the most famous benchmark indicators. As mentioned in *Chapter 1, Deep Learning Overview*, this dataset contains 70,000 handwritten numbers data from 0 to 9, with both a height and width of 28 pixels each.

First, we define the values necessary for the model:

```
int numRows = 28;
int numColumns = 28;
int nChannels = 1;
int outputNum = 10;
int numSamples = 2000;
int batchSize = 500;
int iterations = 10;
int splitTrainNum = (int) (batchSize*.8);
int seed = 123;
int listenerFreq = iterations/5;
```

Since images in MNIST are all grayscale data, the number of channels is set to 1. In this example, we use 2,000 data of 70,000 and split it into training data and test data. The size of the mini-batch is 500 here, so the training data is divided into 4 mini-batches. Furthermore, the data in each mini-batch is split into training data and test data, and each piece of test data is stored in ArrayList:

```
List<INDArray> testInput = new ArrayList<>();
List<INDArray> testLabels = new ArrayList<>();
```

We didn't have to set ArrayList in the previous examples because we had just one batch. For the MnistDataSetIterator class, we can set the MNIST data just by using:

```
DataSetIterator mnistIter = new
MnistDataSetIterator(batchSize,numSamples, true);
```

Then, we build the model with a convolutional layer and subsampling layer. Here, we have one convolutional layer and one max-pooling layer, directly followed by an output layer. The structure of the configurations for CNN is slightly different from the other algorithms:

```
MultiLayerConfiguration.Builder builder = new NeuralNetConfiguration.
Builder().layer().layer(). … .layer()
new ConvolutionLayerSetup(builder,numRows,numColumns,nChannels);
MultiLayerConfiguration conf = builder.build();
MultiLayerNetwork model = new MultiLayerNetwork(conf);
model.init();
```

The difference is that we can't build a model directly from the configuration because we need to tell the builder to set up a convolutional layer using ConvolutionLayerSetup() in advance. Each .layer() requires just the same method of coding. The convolutional layer is defined as:

```
.layer(0, new ConvolutionLayer.Builder(10, 10)
        .stride(2,2)
        .nIn(nChannels)
        .nOut(6)
        .weightInit(WeightInit.XAVIER)
        .activation("relu")
        .build())
```

Here, the value of 10 in `ConvolutionLayer.Builder()` is the size of the kernels, and the value of 6 in `.nOut()` is the number of kernels. Also, `.stride()` defines the size of the strides of the kernels. The code we implemented from scratch in *Chapter 4, Dropout and Convolutional Neural Networks* has a functionality equivalent only to `.stride(1, 1)`. The larger the number is, the less time it takes because it decreases the number of calculations necessary for convolutions, but we have to be careful at the same time that it might also decrease the model's precision. Anyway, we can implement convolutions with more flexibility now.

The `subsampling` layer is described as:

```
.layer(1, new
SubsamplingLayer.Builder(SubsamplingLayer.PoolingType.MAX, new int[]
{2,2})
        .build())
```

Here, `{2, 2}` is the size of the pooling windows. You may have noticed that we don't have to set the size of the inputs for each layer, including the output layer. These values are automatically set once you set up the model.

The output layer can be written just the same as in the other models:

```
.layer(2, new OutputLayer.Builder(LossFunctions.LossFunction.
NEGATIVELOGLIKELIHOOD)
        .nOut(outputNum)
        .weightInit(WeightInit.XAVIER)
        .activation("softmax")
        .build())
```

The graphical model of this example is as follows:

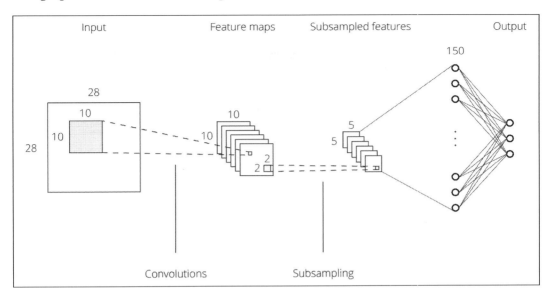

After the building comes the training. Since we have multiple mini-batches, we need to iterate training through all the batches. This can be achieved easily using `.hasNext()` on `DataSetIterator` and `mnistIter` in this case. The whole training process can be written as follows:

```
model.setListeners(Arrays.asList((IterationListener) new ScoreIteratio
nListener(listenerFreq)));
while(mnistIter.hasNext()) {
    mnist = mnistIter.next();
    trainTest = mnist.splitTestAndTrain(splitTrainNum, new
    Random(seed));
    trainInput = trainTest.getTrain();
    testInput.add(trainTest.getTest().getFeatureMatrix());
    testLabels.add(trainTest.getTest().getLabels());
    model.fit(trainInput);
}
```

Here, the test data and test labels are stocked for further use.

During the test, again, we need to iterate the evaluation process of the test data because we have more than one mini-batch:

```
for(int i = 0; i < testInput.size(); i++) {
    INDArray output = model.output(testInput.get(i));
    eval.eval(testLabels.get(i), output);
}
```

Then, we use the same as in the other examples:

```
log.info(eval.stats());
```

This will return the result as follows:

```
==========================Scores=========================================
 Accuracy:   0.832
 Precision:  0.8783
 Recall:     0.8334
 F1 Score:   0.8552464933704985

=========================================================================
```

The example just given is the model with one convolutional layer and one subsampling layer, but you have deep convolutional neural networks with LenetMnistExample.java. In this example, there are two convolutional layers and subsampling layers, followed by fully connected multi-layer perceptrons:

```
MultiLayerConfiguration.Builder builder = new NeuralNetConfiguration.
Builder()
        .seed(seed)
        .batchSize(batchSize)
        .iterations(iterations)
        .regularization(true).l2(0.0005)
        .learningRate(0.01)
        .optimizationAlgo(OptimizationAlgorithm.STOCHASTIC_GRADIENT_
DESCENT)
        .updater(Updater.NESTEROVS).momentum(0.9)
        .list(6)
        .layer(0, new ConvolutionLayer.Builder(5, 5)
                .nIn(nChannels)
                .stride(1, 1)
                .nOut(20).dropOut(0.5)
                .weightInit(WeightInit.XAVIER)
                .activation("relu")
                .build())
```

```
          .layer(1, new
SubsamplingLayer.Builder(SubsamplingLayer.PoolingType.MAX,
new int[]{2, 2})
              .build())
.layer(2, new ConvolutionLayer.Builder(5, 5)
              .nIn(20)
              .nOut(50)
              .stride(2,2)
              .weightInit(WeightInit.XAVIER)
              .activation("relu")
              .build())
.layer(3, new
SubsamplingLayer.Builder(SubsamplingLayer.PoolingType.MAX,
new int[]{2, 2})
              .build())
.layer(4, new DenseLayer.Builder().activation("tanh")
              .nOut(500).build())
.layer(5, new
OutputLayer.Builder(LossFunctions.LossFunction
.NEGATIVELOGLIKELIHOOD)
              .nOut(outputNum)
              .weightInit(WeightInit.XAVIER)
              .activation("softmax")
              .build())
          .backprop(true).pretrain(false);
   new ConvolutionLayerSetup(builder,28,28,1);
```

As you can see in the first convolutional layer, dropout can easily be applied to CNN with DL4J.

With this model, we get the following result:

```
==========================Scores=====================================
 Accuracy:   0.8656
 Precision: 0.8827
 Recall:     0.8645
 F1 Score:   0.873490476878917

=====================================================================
```

You can see from the MNIST dataset page (http://yann.lecun.com/exdb/mnist/) that the state-of-the-art result is much better than the one above. Here, again, you would realize how important the combination of parameters, activation functions, and optimization algorithms are.

Learning rate optimization

We have learned various deep learning algorithms so far; you may have noticed that they have one parameter in common: the learning rate. The learning rate is defined in the equations to update the model parameters. So, why not think of algorithms to optimize the learning rate? Originally, these equations were described as follows:

$$\theta^{(\tau+1)} = \theta^{(\tau)} + \Delta\theta^{(\tau)}$$

Here:

$$\Delta\theta^{(\tau)} = -\eta\frac{\partial E}{\partial\theta^{(\tau)}}$$

Here, τ is the number of steps and η is the learning rate. It is well known that decreasing the value of the learning rate with each iteration lets the model have better precision rates, but we should determine the decline carefully because a sudden drop in the value would collapse the model. The learning rate is one of the model parameters, so why not optimize it? To do so, we need to know what the best rate could be.

The simplest way of setting the rate is using the momentum, represented as follows:

$$\Delta\theta^{(\tau)} = -\eta\frac{\partial E}{\partial\theta^{(\tau)}} + \alpha\Delta\theta^{(\tau-1)}$$

Here, $\alpha \in [0,1]$, called the **momentum coefficient**. This hyper parameter is often set to be 0.5 or 0.9 first and then fine-tuned.

Momentum is actually a simple but effective way of adjusting the learning rate but **ADAGRAD**, proposed by Duchi et al. (`http://www.magicbroom.info/Papers/DuchiHaSi10.pdf`), is known to be a better way. The equation is described as follows:

$$\Delta\theta^{(\tau)} = -\frac{\eta}{\sqrt{\sum_{t=0}^{\tau} g_t^2}} g_\tau$$

Here:

$$g_\tau = \frac{\partial E}{\partial \theta^{(\tau)}}$$

Theoretically, this works well, but practically, we often use the following equations to prevent divergence:

$$\Delta \theta^{(\tau)} = -\frac{\eta}{\sqrt{\sum_{t=0}^{\tau} g_t^2 + 1}} g_\tau$$

Or we use:

$$\Delta \theta^{(\tau)} = -\frac{\eta}{\sqrt{\sum_{t=0}^{\tau} g_t^2 + 1}} g_\tau$$

ADAGRAD is easier to use than momentum because the value is set automatically and we don't have to set additional hyper parameters.

ADADELTA, suggested by Zeiler (`http://arxiv.org/pdf/1212.5701.pdf`), is known to be an even better optimizer. This is an algorithm-based optimizer and cannot be written in a single equation. Here is a description of ADADELTA:

- Initialization:
  - Initialize accumulation variables:

$$E\left[g^2\right]_0 = 0$$

And:

$$E\left[\Delta \theta^2\right]_0 = 0$$

- Iteration $\tau = 0, 1, 2, \ldots, T$:

    ○ Compute:

$$g_\tau = \frac{\partial E}{\partial \theta^{(\tau)}}$$

    ○ Accumulate gradient:

$$E\left[g^2\right]_\tau = \rho E\left[g^2\right]_{\tau-1} + (1-\rho)g_\tau^2$$

    ○ Compute update:

$$\Delta\theta^{(\tau)} = -\frac{\sqrt{E\left[\Delta\theta^2\right]_{\tau-1} + \varepsilon}}{\sqrt{E\left[g^2\right]_\tau + \varepsilon}} g_\tau$$

    ○ Accumulate updates:

$$E\left[\Delta\theta^2\right]_\tau = \rho E\left[\Delta\theta^2\right]_{\tau-1} + (1-\rho)\left(\Delta\theta^{(\tau)}\right)^2$$

    ○ Apply update:

$$\theta^{(\tau+1)} = \theta^{(\tau)} + \Delta\theta^{(\tau)}$$

Here, ρ and ε are the hyper parameters. You may think ADADELTA is rather complicated but you don't need to worry about this complexity when implementing with DL4J.

There are still other optimizers supported in DL4J such as **RMSProp, RMSProp + momentum**, and **Nesterov's Accelerated Gradient Descent**. However, we won't dig into them because, practically, momentum, ADAGRAD, and ADADELTA are enough to optimize the learning rate.

Summary

In this chapter, you learned how to implement deep learning models with the libraries ND4J and DL4J. Both support GPU computing and both give us the ability to implement them without any difficulties. ND4J is a library for scientific computing and enables vectorization, which makes it easier to implement a calculation among arrays because we don't need to write iterations within them. Since machine learning and deep learning algorithms have many equations with vector calculations, such as inner products and element-wise multiplication, ND4J also helps implement them.

DL4J is a library for deep learning, and by following some examples with the library, you saw that we can easily build, train, and evaluate various types of deep learning models. Additionally, while building the model, you learned why regularization is necessary to get better results. You also got to know some optimizers of the learning rate: momentum, ADAGRAD, and ADADELTA. All of these can be implemented easily with DL4J.

You gained knowledge of the core theories and implementations of deep learning algorithms and you now know how to implement them with little difficulty. We can say that we've completed the theoretical part of this book. Therefore, in the next chapter, we'll look at how deep learning algorithms are adapted to practical applications first and then look into other possible fields and ideas to apply the algorithms.

6
Approaches to Practical Applications – Recurrent Neural Networks and More

In the previous chapters, you learned quite a lot about deep learning. You should now understand the fundamentals of the concepts, theories, and implementations of deep neural networks. You also learned that you can experiment with deep learning algorithms on various data relatively easily by utilizing a deep learning library. The next step is to examine how deep learning can be applied to a broad range of other fields and how to utilize it for practical applications.

Therefore, in this chapter, we'll first see how deep learning is actually applied. Here, you will see that the actual cases where deep learning is utilized are still very few. But why aren't there many cases even though it is such an innovative method? What is the problem? Later on, we'll think about the reasons. Furthermore, going forward we will also consider which fields we can apply deep learning to and will have the chance to apply deep learning and all the related areas of artificial intelligence.

The topics covered in this chapter include:

- Image recognition, natural language processing, and the neural networks models and algorithms related to them
- The difficulties of turning deep learning models into practical applications
- The possible fields where deep learning can be applied, and ideas on how to approach these fields

We'll explore the potential of this big AI boom, which will lead to ideas and hints that you can utilize in deep learning for your research, business, and many sorts of activities.

Fields where deep learning is active

We often hear that research for deep learning has always been ongoing and that's a fact. Many corporations, especially large tech companies such as Google, Facebook, Microsoft, and IBM, invest huge amounts of money into the research of deep learning, and we frequently hear news that some corporation has bought these research groups. However, as we look through, deep learning itself has various types of algorithms, and fields where these algorithms can be applied. Even so, it is a fact that is it not widely known which fields deep learning is utilized in or can be used in. Since the word "AI" is so broadly used, people can't properly understand which technology is used for which product. Hence, in this section, we will go through the fields where people have been trying to adopt deep learning actively for practical applications.

Image recognition

The field in which deep learning is most frequently incorporated is image recognition. It was Prof. Hinton and his team's invention that led to the term "deep learning." Their algorithm recorded the lowest error rates ever in an image recognition competition. The continuous research done to improve the algorithm led to even better results. Now, image recognition utilizing deep learning has gradually been adopted not only for studies, but also for practical applications and products. For example, Google utilizes deep learning to auto-generate thumbnails for YouTube or auto-tag and search photos in Google Photos. Like these popular products, deep learning is mainly applied to image tagging or categorizing and, for example, in the field of robotics, it is used for robots to specify things around them.

The reason why we can support these products and this industry is because deep learning is more suited to image processing, and this is because it can achieve higher precision rates than applications in any other field. Only because the precision and recall rate of image recognition is so high does it mean this industry has broad potential. An error rate of MNIST image classification is recorded at 0.21 percent with a deep learning algorithm (http://cs.nyu.edu/~wanli/dropc/), and this rate can be no lower than the record for a human (http://arxiv.org/pdf/0710.2231v1.pdf). In other words, if you narrow it down to just image recognition, it's nothing more than the fact that a machine may overcome a human. Why does only image recognition get such high precision while other fields need far more improvement in their methods?

One of the reasons is that the structure of feature extractions in deep learning is well suited for image data. In deep neural networks, many layers are stacked and features are extracted from training data step by step at each layer. Also, it can be said that image data is featured as a layered structure. When you look at images, you will unconsciously catch brief features first and then look into a more detailed feature. Therefore, the inherent property of deep learning feature extraction is similar to how an image is perceived and hence we can get an accurate realization of the features. Although image recognition with deep learning still needs more improvements, especially of how machines can understand images and their contents, obtaining high precision by just adopting deep learning to sample image data without preprocessing obviously means that deep learning and image data are a good match.

The other reason is that people have been working to improve algorithms slowly but steadily. For example, in deep learning algorithms, CNN, which can get the best precision for image recognition, has been improved every time it faces difficulties/tasks. Local receptive fields substituted with kernels of convolutional layers were introduced to avoid networks becoming too dense. Also, downsampling methods such as max-pooling were invented to avoid the overreaction of networks towards a gap of image location. This was originally generated from a trial and error process on how to recognize handwritten letters written in a certain frame such as a postal code. As such, there are many cases where a new approach is sought to adapt neural networks algorithms for practical applications. A complicated model, CNN is also built based on these accumulated yet steady improvements. While we don't need feature engineering with deep learning, we still need to consider an appropriate approach to solve specific problems, that is, we can't build omnipotent models, and this is known as the **No Free Lunch Theorem (NFLT)** for optimization.

In the image recognition field, the classification accuracy that can be achieved by deep learning is extremely high, and it is actually beginning to be used for practical applications. However, there should be more fields where deep learning can be applied. Images have a close connection to many industries. In the future, there will be many cases and many more industries that utilize deep learning. In this book, let's think about what industries we can apply image recognition to, considering the emergence of deep learning in the next sections.

Natural language processing

The second most active field, after image recognition, where the research of deep learning has progressed is **natural language processing** (NLP). The research in this field might become the most active going forward. With regard to image recognition, the prediction precision we could obtain almost reaches the ceiling, as it can perform even better classification than a human could. On the other hand, in NLP, it is true that the performance of a model gets a lot better thanks to deep learning, but it is also a fact that there are many tasks that still need to be solved.

For some products and practical applications, deep learning has already been applied. For example, NLP based on deep learning is applied to Google's voice search or voice recognition and Google translation. Also, IBM Watson, the cognitive computing system that understands and learns natural language and supports human decision-making, extracts keywords and entities from tons of documents, and has functions to label documents. And these functions are open to the public as the Watson API and anyone can utilize it without constraints.

As you can see from the preceding examples, NLP itself has a broad and varied range of types. In terms of fundamental techniques, we have the classification of sentence contents, the classification of words, and the specification of word meanings. Furthermore, languages such as Chinese or Japanese that don't leave a space between words require morphological analysis, which is also another technique available in NLP.

NLP contains a lot of things that need to be researched, therefore it needs to clarify what its purpose is, what its problems are, and how these problems can be solved. What model is the best to use and how to get good precision properly are topics that should be examined cautiously. As for image recognition, the CNN method was invented by solving tasks that were faced. Now, let's consider what approach we can think of and what the difficulties will be respectively for neural networks and NLP. Understanding past trial and error processes will be useful for research and applications going forward.

Feed-forward neural networks for NLP

The fundamental problem of NLP is "to predict the next word given a specific word or words". The problem is too simple, however; if you try to solve it with neural networks, then you will soon face several difficulties because documents or sentences as sample data using NLP have the following features:

- The length of each sentence is not fixed but variable, and the number of words is astronomical

- There can be unforeseen problems such as misspelled words, acronyms, and so on

- Sentences are sequential data, and so contain temporal information

Why can these features pose a problem? Remember the model structure of general neural networks. For training and testing with neural networks, the number of neurons in each layer including the input layer needs to be fixed in advance and the networks need to be the same size for all the sample data. In the meantime, the length of the input data is not fixed and can vary a lot. This means that sample data cannot be applied to the model, at least as it is. Classification or generation by neural networks cannot be done without adding/amending something to this data.

We have to fix the length of input data, and one approach to handle this issue is a method that divides a sentence into a chunk of certain words from the beginning in order. This method is called **N-gram**. Here, *N* represents the size of each item, and an **N-gram** of size 1 is called a **unigram**, size 2 is a **bigram**, and size 3 is a **trigram**. When the size is larger, then it is simply called with the value of *N*, such as *four-gram*, *five-gram*, and so on.

Let's look at how N-gram works with NLP. The goal here is to calculate the probability of a word w given some history h; $P(w|h)$. We'll represent a sequence of N words as w_1^n. Then, the probability we want to compute is $P(w_1^n)$, and by applying the chain rule of probability to this term, we get:

$$P(w_1^n) = P(w_1)P(w_2 \mid w_3)P(w_3 \mid w_1^2)...P(w_n \mid w_1^{n-1})$$

$$= \prod_{k=1}^{n} P(w_k \mid w_1^{k-1})$$

It might look at first glance like these conditional probabilities help us, but actually they don't because we have no way of calculating the exact probability of a word following a long sequence of preceding words, $P(w_n \mid w_{n-1})$. Since the structure of a sentence is very flexible, we can't simply utilize sample documents and a corpus to estimate the probability. This is where N-gram works. Actually, we have two approaches to solve this problem: the original N-gram model and the neural networks model based on N-gram. We'll look at the first one to fully understand how the fields of NLP have developed before we dig into neural networks.

With N-gram, we don't compute the probability of a word given its whole history, but approximate the history with the last N words. For example, the bigram model approximates the probability of a word just by the conditional probability of the preceding word, $P(w_n \mid w_{n-1})$, and so follows the equation:

$$P(w_1^n) = \prod_{k=1}^{n} P(w_k \mid w_1^{k-1})$$

$$\approx \prod_{k=1}^{n} P(w_k \mid w_{k-1})$$

Similarly, we can generalize and expand the equation for N-gram. In this case, the probability of a word can be represented as follows:

$$P(w_n \mid w_1^{n-1}) \approx P(w_n \mid w_{n-N+1}^{n-1})$$

We get the following equation:

$$P(w_1^n) \approx \prod_{k=1}^{n} P(w_k \mid w_{k-N+1}^{k-1})$$

Just bear in mind that these approximations with N-gram are based on the probabilistic model called the **Markov model**, where the probability of a word depends only on the previous word.

Now what we need to do is estimate these N-gram probabilities, but how do we estimate them? One simple way of doing this is called the **maximum likelihood estimation** (**MLE**). This method estimates the probabilities by taking counts from a corpus and normalizing them. So when we think of a bigram as an example, we get:

$$P\left(w_n \mid w_{n-1}\right) = \frac{C\left(w_{n-1}w_n\right)}{\sum_w C\left(w_{n-1}w\right)}$$

In the preceding formula, $C(\cdot)$ denotes the counts of a word or a sequence of words. Since the denominator, that is, the sum of all bigram counts starting with a word, w_{n-1} is equal to the unigram count of w_{n-1}, the preceding equation can be described as follows:

$$P\left(w_n \mid w_{n-1}\right) = \frac{C\left(w_{n-1}w_n\right)}{C\left(w_{n-1}\right)}$$

Accordingly, we can generalize MLE for N-gram as well:

$$P\left(w_n \mid w_{n-N+1}^{n-1}\right) = \frac{C\left(w_{n-N+1}^{n-1}w_n\right)}{C\left(w_{n-N+1}^{n-1}\right)}$$

Although this is a fundamental approach of NLP with N-gram, we now know how to compute N-gram probabilities.

In contrast to this approach, the neural network models predict the conditional probability of a word w_j given a specific history, h_j; $P\left(w_j = i \mid h_j\right)$. One of the models of NLP is called the **Neural Network Language Model (NLMM)** (http://www.jmlr.org/papers/volume3/bengio03a/bengio03a.pdf), and it can be illustrated as follows:

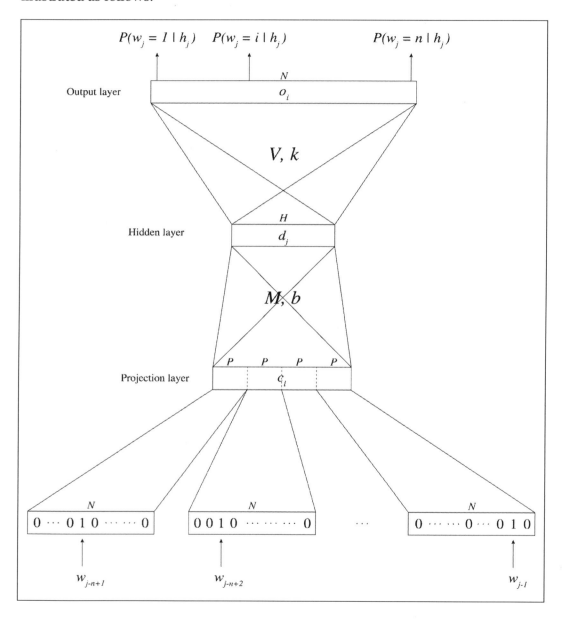

Here, N is the size of the vocabulary, and each word in the vocabulary is an N-dimensional vector where only the index of the word is set to 1 and all the other indices to 0. This method of representation is called *1-of-N coding*. The inputs of NLMM are the indices of the $n-1$ previous words $h_j = w_{j-n+1}^{j-1}$ (so they are *n-grams*). Since the size N is typically within the range of 5,000 to 200,000, input vectors of NLMM are very sparse. Then, each word is mapped to the projection layer, for continuous space representation. This linear projection (activation) from a discrete to a continuous space is basically a look-up table with $N \times P$ entries, where P denotes the feature dimension. The projection matrix is shared for the different word positions in the context, and activates the word vectors to projection layer units c_l with $l = 1,\ldots,(n-1).P$. After the projection comes the hidden layer. Since the projection layer is in the continuous space, the model structure is just the same as the other neural networks from here. So, the activation can be represented as follows:

$$d_j = h\left(\sum_{l=1}^{(n-1).P} m_{jl}c_l + b_j \right)$$

Here, $h(\cdot)$ denotes the activation function, m_{ji} the weights between the projection layer and the hidden layer, and b_j the biases of the hidden layer. Accordingly, we can get the output units as follows:

$$o_i = \sum_j v_{ij}d_j + k_i$$

Here, v_{ij} denotes the weights between the hidden layer and the output layer, and k_i denotes the biases of the output layer. The probability of a word i given a specific history h_j can then be calculated using the softmax function:

$$P\left(w_j = i \mid h_j\right) = \frac{\exp\left(o_i\right)}{\sum_{l=1}^{N} \exp\left(o_i\right)}$$

As you can see, in NNLM, the model predicts the probability of all the words at the same time. Since the model is now described with the standard neural network, we can train the model using the standard backpropagation algorithm.

NNLM is one approach of NLP using neural networks with N-gram. Though NNLM solves the problem of how to fix the number of inputs, the best N can only be found by trial and error, and it is the most difficult part of the whole model building process. In addition, we have to make sure that we don't put too much weight on the temporal information of the inputs here.

Deep learning for NLP

Neural networks with N-gram may work with certain cases, but contain some issues, such as what n-grams would return the best results, and do n-grams, the inputs of the model, still have a context? These are the problems not only of NLP, but of all the other fields that have time sequential data such as precipitation, stock prices, yearly crop of potatoes, movies, and so on. Since we have such a massive amount of this data in the real world, we can't ignore the potential issue. But then, how would it be possible to let neural networks be trained with time sequential data?

Recurrent neural networks

One of the neural network models that is able to preserve the context of data within networks is **recurrent neural network (RNN)**, the model that actively studies the evolution of deep learning algorithms. The following is a very simple graphical model of RNN:

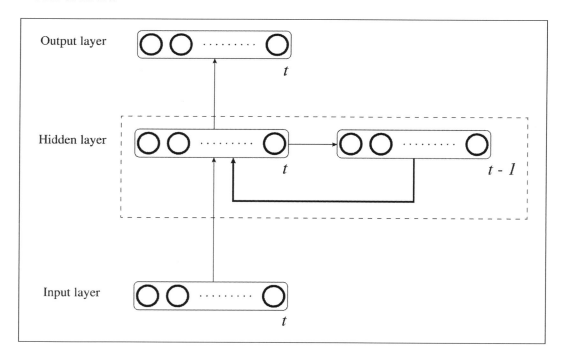

The difference between standard neural networks is that RNN has connections between hidden layers with respect to time. The input at time t is activated in the hidden layer at time t, preserved in the hidden layer, and then propagated to the hidden layer at time $t+1$ with the input at time $t+1$. This enables the networks to contain the states of past data and reflect them. You might think that RNN is rather a dynamic model, but if you unfold the model at each time step, you can see that RNN is a static model:

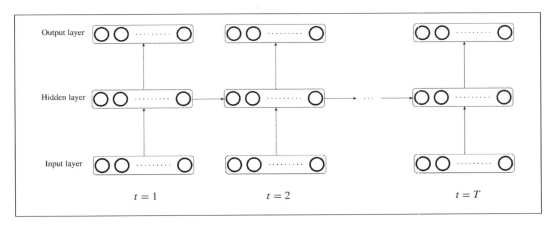

Since the model structure at each time step is the same as in general neural networks, you can train this model using the backpropagation algorithm. However, you need to consider time relevance when training, and there is a technique called **Backpropagation through Time (BPTT)** to handle this. In BPTT, the errors and gradients of the parameter are backpropagated to the layers of the past:

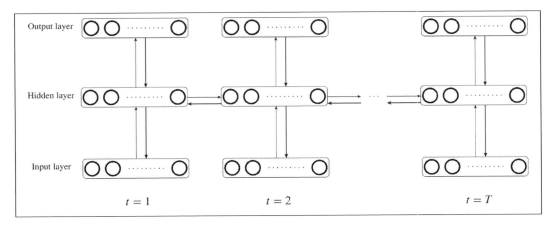

Thus, RNN can preserve contexts within the model. Theoretically, the network at each time step should consider the whole sequence up to then, but practically, time windows with a certain length are often applied to the model to make the calculation less complicated or to prevent the vanishing gradient problem and the exploding gradient problem. BPTT has enabled training among layers and this is why RNN is often considered to be one of the deep neural networks. We also have algorithms of deep RNN such as stacked RNN where hidden layers are stacked.

RNN has been adapted for NLP, and is actually one of the most successful models in this field. The original model optimized for NLP is called the **recurrent neural network language model (RNNLM)**, introduced by Mikolov et al. (`http://www.fit.vutbr.cz/research/groups/speech/publi/2010/mikolov_interspeech2010_IS100722.pdf`). The model architecture can be illustrated as follows:

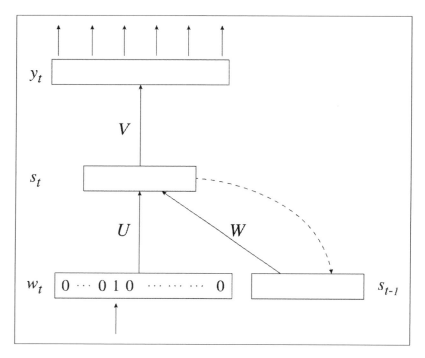

The network has three layers: an input layer x, a hidden layer s, and an output layer y. The hidden layer is also often called the context layer or the state layer. The value of each layer with respect to the time t can be represented as follows:

$$x_t = w_t + s_{t-1}$$
$$s_t = f\left(Uw_t + Ws_{t-1}\right)$$
$$y_t = g\left(Vs_t\right)$$

Here, $f(\cdot)$ denotes the sigmoid function, and $g(\cdot)$ the softmax function. Since the input layer contains the state layer at time $t-1$, it can reflect the whole context to the network. The model architecture implies that RNNLM can look up much broader contexts than feed-forward NNLM, in which the length of the context is constrained to N (-gram).

The whole time and the entire context should be considered while training RNN, but as mentioned previously, we often truncate the time length because BPTT requires a lot of calculations and often causes the gradient vanishing/exploding problem when learning long-term dependencies, hence the algorithm is often called **truncated BPTT**. If we unfold RNNLM with respect to time, the model can be illustrated as follows (in the figure, the unfolded time $\tau = 3$):

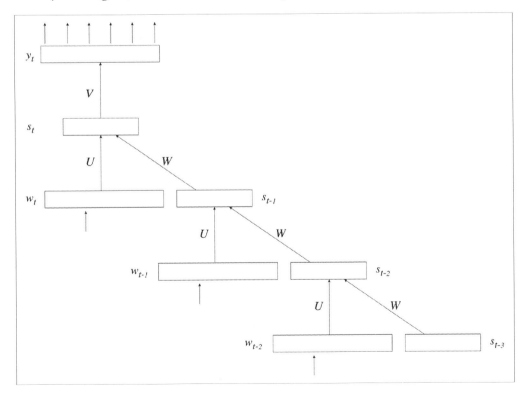

Here d_t is the label vector of the output. Then, the error vector of the output can be represented as follows:

$$\delta_t^{out} = d_t - y_t$$

We get the following equation:

$$\delta_t^{hidden} = d\left(\left(\delta_t^{out}\right)^T V, t\right)$$

Here T is the unfolding time:

$$d(x,t) = xs_t \left(1 - s_t\right)$$

The preceding image is the derivative of the activation function of the hidden layer. Since we use the sigmoid function here, we get the preceding equation. Then, we can get the error of the past as follows:

$$\delta_{t-\tau-1}^{hidden} = d\left(\left(\delta_{t-\tau}^{out}\right)^T V, t-\tau-1\right)$$

With these equations, we can now update the weight matrices of the model:

$$V_{t+1} = V_t + s_t \left(\delta_t^{out}\right)^T \alpha$$

$$U_{t+1} = U_t + \sum_{\tau=0}^{T} w_{t-\tau} \left(\delta_{t-\tau}^{hidden}\right)^T \alpha$$

$$W_{t+1} = W_t + \sum_{\tau=0}^{T} w_{t-\tau-1} \left(\delta_{t-\tau}^{hidden}\right)^T \alpha$$

Here, α is the learning rate. What is interesting in RNNLM is that each vector in the matrix shows the difference between words after training. This is because U is the matrix that maps each word to a latent space, so after the training, mapped word vectors contain the meaning of the words. For example, the vector calculation of "king" – "man" + "woman" would return "queen". DL4J supports RNN, so you can easily implement this model with the library.

Long short term memory networks

Training with the standard RNN requires the truncated BPTT. You might well doubt then that BPTT can really train the model enough to reflect the whole context, and this is very true. This is why a special kind of RNN, the **long short term memory (LSTM)** network, was introduced to solve the long-term dependency problem. LSTM is rather intimidating, but let's briefly explore the concept of LSTM.

To begin with, we have to think about how we can store and tell past information in the network. While the gradient exploding problem can be mitigated simply by setting a ceiling to the connection, the gradient vanishing problem still needs to be deeply considered. One possible approach is to introduce a unit that permanently preserves the value of its inputs and its gradient. So, when you look at a unit in the hidden layer of standard neural networks, it is simply described as follows:

There's nothing special here. Then, by adding a unit below to the network, the network can now memorize the past information within the neuron. The neuron added here has linear activation and its value is often set to 1. This neuron, or cell, is called **constant error carousel (CEC)** because the error stays in the neuron like a carousel and won't vanish. CEC works as a storage cell and stores past inputs. This solves the gradient vanishing problem, but raises another problem. Since all data propagated through is stocked in the neuron, it probably stores noise data as well:

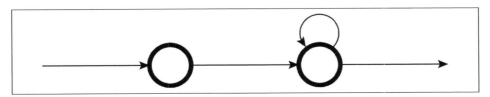

This problem can be broken down into two problems: *input weight conflicts* and *output weight conflicts*. The key idea of input weight conflicts is to keep certain information within the network until it's necessary; the neuron is to be activated only when the relevant information comes, but is not to be activated otherwise. Similarly, output weight conflicts can occur in all types of neural networks; the value of neurons is to be propagated only when necessary, and not to be propagated otherwise. We can't solve these problems as long as the connection between neurons is represented with the weight of the network. Therefore, another method or technique of representation is required that controls the propagation of inputs and outputs. But how do we do this? The answer is putting units that act like "gates" before and behind the CEC, and these are called **input gate** and **output gate**, respectively. The graphical model of the gate can be described as follows:

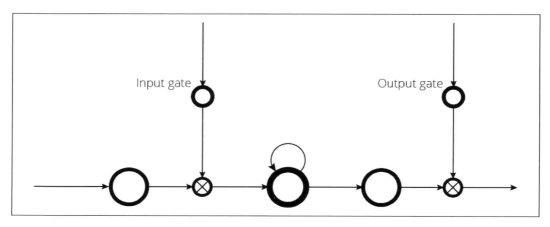

Ideally, the gate should return the discrete value of 0 or 1 corresponding to the input, 0 when the gate is closed and 1 when open, because it is a gate, but programmatically, the gate is set to return the value in the range of 0 to 1 so that it can be well trained with BPTT.

It may seem like we can now put and fetch exact information at an exact time, yet another problem still remains. With just two gates, the input gate and output gate, memories stored in the CEC can't be refreshed easily in a few steps. Therefore, we need an additional gate that dynamically changes the value of the CEC. To do this, we add a **forget gate** to the architecture to control when the memory should be erased. The value preserved in the CEC is overridden with a new memory when the value of the gate takes a 0 or close to it. With these three gates, a unit can now memorize information or contexts of the past, and so it is called an **LSTM block** or an **LSTM memory block** because it is more of a block than a single neuron. The following is a figure that represents an LSTM block:

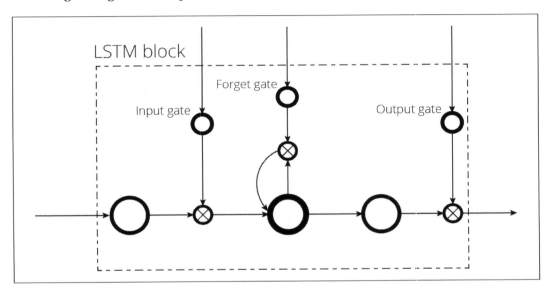

The standard LSTM structure was fully explained previously, but there's a technique to get better performance from it, which we'll explain now. Each gate receives connections from the input units and the outputs of all the units in LSTM, but there is no direct connection from the CEC. This means we can't see the true hidden state of the network because the output of a block depends so much on the output gate; as long as the output gate is closed, none of the gates can access the CEC and it is devoid of essential information, which may debase the performance of LSTM. One simple yet effective solution is to add connections from the CEC to the gates in a block. These are called **peephole connections**, and act as standard weighted connections except that no errors are backpropagated from the gates through the peephole connections. The peephole connections let all gates assume the hidden state even when the output gate is closed. You've learned a lot of terms now, but as a result, the basic architecture of the whole connection can be described as follows:

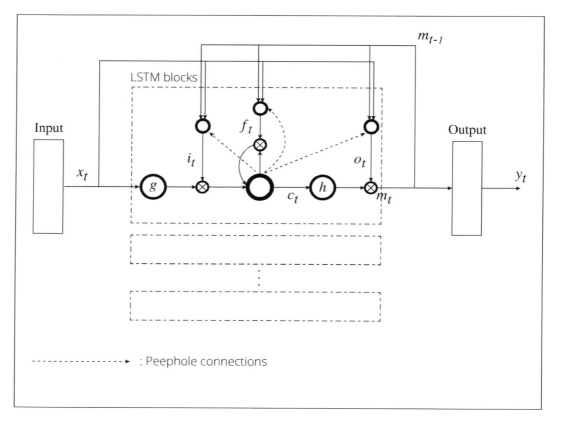

For simplicity, a single LSTM block is described in the figure. You might be daunted because the preceding model is very intricate. However, when you look at the model step by step, you can understand how an LSTM network has figured out how to overcome difficulties in NLP. Given an input sequence $x = (x_1, \ldots, x_T)$, each network unit can be calculated as follows:

$$i_t = \sigma \left(W_{ix} x_t + W_{im} m_{t-1} + W_{ic} c_{t-1} + b_i \right)$$

$$f_t = \sigma \left(W_{fx} x_t + W_{fm} m_{t-1} + W_{fc} c_{t-1} + b_f \right)$$

$$c_t = f_t \odot c_{t-1} + i_t \odot g \left(W_{cx} x_t + W_{cm} m_{t-1} + b_c \right)$$

$$o_t = \sigma \left(W_{ox} x_t + W_{om} m_{t-1} + W_{oc} c_t + b_o \right)$$

$$m_t = o_t \odot h \left(c_t \right)$$

$$y_t = s \left(W_{ym} m_t + b_y \right)$$

In the preceding formulas, W_{ix} is the matrix of weights from the input gate to the input, W_{ix} is the one from the forget gate to the input, and W_{ox} is the one from the output gate to the input. W_{cs} is the weight matrix from the cell to the input, W_{cm} is the one from the cell to the LSTM output, and W_{ym} is the one from the output to the LSTM output. W_{ic}, W_{fc}, and W_{oc} are diagonal weight matrices for peephole connections. The b terms denote the bias vectors, b_i is the input gate bias vector, b_f is the forget gate bias vector, b_o is the output gate bias vector, b_c is the CEC cell bias vector, and b_y is the output bias vector. Here, g and h are activation functions of the cell input and cell output. σ denotes the sigmoid function, and $s(\cdot)$ the softmax function. $\odot$ is the element-wise product of the vectors.

We won't follow the further math equations in this book because they become too complicated just by applying BPTT, but you can try LSTM with DL4J as well as RNN. As CNN was developed within the field of image recognition, RNN and LSTM have been developed to resolve the issues of NLP that arise one by one. While both algorithms are just one approach to get a better performance using NLP and still need to be improved, since we are living beings that communicate using languages, the development of NLP will certainly lead to technological innovations. For applications of LSTM, you can reference *Sequence to Sequence Learning with Neural Networks* (Sutskever et al., `http://arxiv.org/pdf/1409.3215v3.pdf`), and for more recent algorithms, you can reference *Grid Long Short-Term Memory* (Kalchbrenner et al., `http://arxiv.org/pdf/1507.01526v1.pdf`) and *Show, Attend and Tell: Neural Image Caption Generation with Visual Attention* (Xu et al., `http://arxiv.org/pdf/1502.03044v2.pdf`).

The difficulties of deep learning

Deep learning has already got higher precision than humans in the image recognition field and has been applied to quite a lot of practical applications. Similarly, in the NLP field, many models have been researched. Then, how much deep learning is utilized in other fields? Surprisingly, there are still few fields where deep learning is successfully utilized. This is because deep learning is indeed innovative compared to past algorithms and definitely lets us take a big step towards materializing AI; however, it has some problems when used for practical applications.

The first problem is that there are too many model parameters in deep learning algorithms. We didn't look in detail when you learned about the theory and implementation of algorithms, but actually deep neural networks have many hyper parameters that need to be decided compared to the past neural networks or other machine learning algorithms. This means we have to go through more trial and error to get high precision. Combinations of parameters that define a structure of neural networks, such as how many hidden layers are to be set or how many units each hidden layer should have, need lots of experiments. Also, the parameters for training and test configurations such as the learning rate need to be determined. Furthermore, peculiar parameters for each algorithm such as the corruption level in SDA and the size of kernels in CNN need additional trial and error. Thus, the great performance that deep learning provides is supported by steady parameter-tuning. However, people only look at one side of deep learning—that it can get great precision— and they tend to forget the hard process required to reach that point. Deep learning is not magic.

In addition, deep learning often fails to train and classify data from simple problems. The shape of deep neural networks is so deep and complicated that the weights can't be well optimized. In terms of optimization, data quantities are also important. This means that deep neural networks require a significant amount of time for each training. To sum up, deep learning shows its worth when:

- It solves complicated and hard problems when people have no idea what feature they can be classified as

- There is sufficient training data to properly optimize deep neural networks

Compared to applications that constantly update a model using continuously updated data, once a model is built using a large-scale dataset that doesn't change drastically, applications that use the model universally are rather well suited for deep learning.

Therefore, when you look at business fields, you can say that there are more cases where the existing machine learning can get better results than using deep learning. For example, let's assume we would like to recommend appropriate products to users in an EC. In this EC, many users buy a lot of products daily, so purchase data is largely updated daily. In this case, do you use deep learning to get high-precision classification and recommendations to increase the conversion rates of users' purchases using this data? Probably not, because using the existing machine learning algorithms such as Naive Bayes, collaborative filtering, SVM, and so on, we can get sufficient precision from a practical perspective and can update the model and calculate quicker, which is usually more appreciated. This is why deep learning is not applied much in business fields. Of course, getting higher precision is better in any field, but in reality, higher precision and the necessary calculation time are in a trade-off relationship. Although deep learning is significant in the research field, it has many hurdles yet to clear considering practical applications.

Besides, deep learning algorithms are not perfect, and they still need many improvements to their model itself. For example, RNN, as mentioned earlier, can only satisfy either how past information can be reflected to a network or how precision can be obtained, although it's contrived with techniques such as LSTM. Also, deep learning is still far from the true AI, although it's definitely a great technique compared to the past algorithms. Research on algorithms is progressing actively, but in the meantime, we need one more breakthrough to spread out and infiltrate deep learning into broader society. Maybe this is not just the problem of a model. Deep learning is suddenly booming because it is reinforced by huge developments in hardware and software. Deep learning is closely related to development of the surrounding technology.

As mentioned earlier, there are still many hurdles to clear before deep learning can be applied more practically in the real world, but this is not impossible to achieve. It isn't possible to suddenly invent AI to achieve technological singularity, but there are some fields and methods where deep learning can be applied right away. In the next section, we'll think about what kinds of industries deep learning can be utilized in. Hopefully, it will sow the seeds for new ideas in your business or research fields.

The approaches to maximizing deep learning possibilities and abilities

There are several approaches to how we can apply deep learning to various industries. While it is true that an approach could be different depending on the task or purpose, we can briefly categorize the approaches in the following three ways:

- **Field-oriented approach**: This utilizes deep learning algorithms or models that are already thoroughly researched and can lead to great performance

- **Breakdown-oriented approach**: This replaces the problems to be solved that deep learning can apparently be applied to with a different problem where deep learning can be well adopted

- **Output-oriented approach**: This explores new ways of how we express the output with deep learning

These approaches are all explained in detail in the following subsections. Each approach is divided into its suitable industries or areas where it is not suitable, but any of them could be a big hint for your activities going forward. There are still very few use cases of deep learning and bias against fields of use, but this means there should be many chances to create innovative and new things. Start-ups that utilize deep learning have been emerging recently and some of them have already achieved success to some extent. You can have a significant impact on the world depending on your ideas.

Field-oriented approach

This approach doesn't require new techniques or algorithms. There are obviously fields that are well suited to the current deep learning techniques, and the concept here is to dive into these fields. As explained previously, since deep learning algorithms that have been practically studied and developed are mostly in image recognition and NLP, we'll explore some fields that can work in great harmony with them.

Medicine

Medical fields should be developed by deep learning. Tumors or cancers are detected on scanned images. This means nothing more than being able to utilize one of the strongest features of deep learning—the technique of image recognition. It is possible to dramatically increase precision using deep learning to help with the early detection of an illness and identifying the kind of illness. Since CNN can be applied to 3D images, 3D scanned images should be able to be analyzed relatively easily. By adopting deep learning more in the current medical field, deep learning should greatly contribute.

We can also say that deep learning can be significantly useful for the medical field in the future. The medical field has been under strict regulations; however, there is a movement progressing to ease the regulations in some countries, probably because of the recent development of IT and its potential. Therefore, there will be opportunities in business for the medical field and IT to have a synergistic effect. For example, if telemedicine is more infiltrated, there is the possibility that diagnosing or identifying a disease can be done not only by a scanned image, but also by an image shown in real time on a display. Also, if electronic charts become widespread, it would be easier to analyze medical data using deep learning. This is because medical records are compatible with deep learning as they are a dataset of texts and images. Then the symptoms of unknown diseases can be found.

Automobiles

We can say that the surroundings of running cars are image sequences and text. Other cars and views are images and a road sign has text. This means we can also utilize deep learning techniques here, and it is possible to reduce the risk of accidents by improving driving assistance functions. It can be said that the ultimate type of driving assistance is self-driving cars, which is being tackled mainly by Google and Tesla. An example that is both famous and fascinating was when George Hotz, the first person to hack the iPhone, built a self-driving car in his garage. The appearance of the car was introduced in an article by Bloomberg Business (`http://www.bloomberg.com/features/2015-george-hotz-self-driving-car/`), and the following image was included in the article:

Self-driving cars have been already tested in the U.S., but since other countries have different traffic rules and road conditions, this idea requires further studying and development before self-driving cars are commonly used worldwide. The key to success in this field is in learning and recognizing surrounding cars, people, views, and traffic signs, and properly judging how to process them.

In the meantime, we don't have to just focus on utilizing deep learning techniques for the actual body of a car. Let's assume we could develop a smartphone app that has the same function as we just described, that is, recognizing and classifying surrounding images and text. Then, if you just set up the smartphone in your car, you could utilize it as a car-navigation app. In addition, for example, it could be used as a navigation app for blind people, providing them with good, reliable directions.

Advert technologies

Advert (ad) technologies could expand their coverage with deep learning. When we say ad technologies, this currently means recommendation or ad networks that optimize ad banners or products to be shown. On the other hand, when we say advertising, this doesn't only mean banners or ad networks. There are various kinds of ads in the world depending on the type of media, such as TV ads, radio ads, newspaper ads, posters, flyers, and so on. We have also digital ad campaigns with YouTube, Vine, Facebook, Twitter, Snapchat, and so on. Advertising itself has changed its definition and content, but all ads have one thing in common: they consist of images and/or language. This means they are fields that deep learning is good at. Until now, we could only use user-behavior-based indicators, such as **page view (PV)**, **click through rate (CTR)**, and **conversion rate (CVR)**, to estimate the effect of an ad, but if we apply deep learning technologies, we might be able to analyze the actual content of an ad and autogenerate ads going forward. Especially since movies and videos can only be analyzed as a result of image recognition and NLP, video recognition, not image recognition, will gather momentum besides ad technologies.

Profession or practice

Professions such as doctor, lawyer, patent attorney, and accountant are considered to be roles that deep learning can replace. For example, if NLP's precision and accuracy gets higher, any perusal that requires expertise can be left to a machine. As a machine can cover these time-consuming reading tasks, people can focus more on high-value tasks. In addition, if a machine classifies past judicial cases or medical cases on what disease caused what symptoms and so on, we would be able to build an app like Apple's Siri that answers simple questions that usually require professional knowledge. Then the machine could handle these professional cases to some extent if a doctor or a lawyer is too busy to help in a timely manner.

It's often said that AI takes away a human's job, but personally, this seems incorrect. Rather, a machine takes away menial work, which should support humans. A software engineer who works on AI programming can be described as having a professional job, but this work will also be changed in the future. For example, think about a car-related job, where the current work is building standard automobiles, but in the future, engineers will be in a position just like pit crews for Formula 1 cars.

Sports

Deep learning can certainly contribute to sports as well. In the study field known as sports science, it has become increasingly important to analyze and examine data from sports. As an example, you may know the book or movie *Moneyball*. In this film, they hugely increased the win percentage of the team by adopting a regression model in baseball. Watching sports itself is very exciting, but on the other hand, sport can be seen as a chunk of image sequences and number data. Since deep learning is good at identifying features that humans can't find, it will become easier to find out why certain players get good scores while others don't.

These fields we have mentioned are only a small part of the many fields where deep learning is capable of significantly contributing to development. We have looked into these fields from the perspective of whether a field has images or text, but of course deep learning should also show great performance for simple analysis with general number data. It should be possible to apply deep learning to various other fields, such as bioinformatics, finance, agriculture, chemistry, astronomy, economy, and more.

Breakdown-oriented approach

This approach might be similar to the approach considered in traditional machine learning algorithms. We already talked about how feature engineering is the key to improving precision in machine learning. Now we can say that this feature engineering can be divided into the following two parts:

- Engineering under the constraints of a machine learning model. The typical case is to make inputs discrete or continuous.

- Feature engineering to increase precision by machine learning. This tends to rely on the sense of a researcher.

In a narrower meaning, feature engineering is considered as the second one, and this is the part that deep learning doesn't have to focus on, whereas the first one is definitely the important part, even for deep learning. For example, it's difficult to predict stock prices using deep learning. Stock prices are volatile and it's difficult to define inputs. Besides, how to apply an output value is also a difficult problem. Enabling deep learning to handle these inputs and outputs is also said to be feature engineering in the wider sense. If there is no limitation to the value of original data and/or data you would like to predict, it's difficult to insert these datasets into machine learning and deep learning algorithms, including neural networks.

However, we can take a certain approach and apply a model to these previous problems by breaking down the inputs and/or outputs. In terms of NLP, as explained earlier, you might have thought, for example, that it would be impossible to put numberless words into features in the first place, but as you already know, we can train feed-forward neural networks with words by representing them with sparse vectors and combining N-grams into them. Of course, we can not only use neural networks, but also other machine learning algorithms such as SVM here. Thus, we can cultivate a new field where deep learning hasn't been applied by engineering to fit features well into deep learning models. In the meantime, when we focus on NLP, we can see that RNN and LSTM were developed to properly resolve the difficulties or tasks encountered in NLP. This can be considered as the opposite approach to feature engineering because in this case, the problem is solved by breaking down a model to fit into features.

Then, how do we do utilize engineering for stock prediction as we just mentioned? It's actually not difficult to think of inputs, that is, features. For example, if you predict stock prices daily, it's hard to calculate if you use daily stock prices as features, but if you use a rate of price change between a day and the day before, then it should be much easier to process as the price stays within a certain range and the gradients won't explode easily. Meanwhile, what is difficult is how to deal with outputs. Stock prices are of course continuous values, hence outputs can be various values. This means that in the neural network model where the number of units in the output layer is fixed, they can't handle this problem. What should we do here—should we give up?! No, wait a minute. Unfortunately, we can't predict a stock price itself, but there is an alternative prediction method.

Here, the problem is that we can classify stock prices to be predicted into infinite patterns. Then, can we make them into limited patterns? Yes, we can. Let's forcibly make them. Think about the most extreme but easy to understand case: predicting whether tomorrow's stock price, strictly speaking a close price, is up or down using the data from the stock price up to today. For this case, we can show it with a deep learning model as follows:

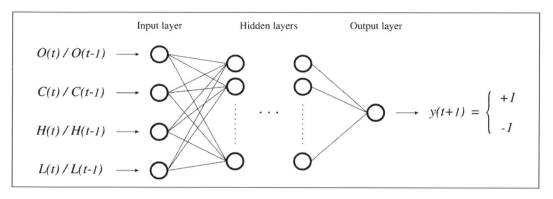

In the preceding image, $o(t)$ denotes the open price of a day, t; $c(t)$ denotes the close price, $H(t)$ is the high price, and $L(t)$ is the actual price. The features used here are mere examples, and need to be fine-tuned when applied to real applications. The point here is that replacing the original task with this type of problem enables deep neural networks to theoretically classify data. Furthermore, if you classify the data by how much it will go up or down, you could make more detailed predictions. For example, you could classify data as shown in the following table:

Class	Description
Class 1	Up more than 3 percent from the closing price
Class 2	Up more than 1~3 percent from the closing price
Class 3	Up more than 0~1 percent from the closing price
Class 4	Down more than 0~-1 percent from the closing price
Class 5	Down more than -1~-3 percent from the closing price
Class 6	Down more than -3 percent from the closing price

Whether the prediction actually works, in other words whether the classification works, is unknown until we examine it, but the fluctuation of stock prices can be predicted in quite a narrow range by dividing the outputs into multiple classes. Once we can adopt the task into neural networks, then what we should do is just examine which model gets better results. In this example, we may apply RNN because the stock price is time sequential data. If we look at charts showing the price as image data, we can also use CNN to predict the future price.

So now we've thought about the approach by referring to examples, but to sum up in general, we can say that:

- **Feature engineering for models**: This is designing inputs or adjusting values to fit deep learning models, or enabling classification by setting a limitation for the outputs
- **Model engineering for features**: This is devising new neural network models or algorithms to solve problems in a focused field

The first one needs ideas for the part of designing inputs and outputs to fit to a model, whereas the second one needs to take a mathematical approach. Feature engineering might be easier to start if you are conscious of making an item prediction-limited.

Output-oriented approach

The two previously mentioned approaches are to increase the percentage of correct answers for a certain field's task or problem using deep learning. Of course, it is essential and the part where deep learning proves its worth; however, increasing precision to the ultimate level may not be the only way of utilizing deep learning. Another approach is to devise the outputs using deep learning by slightly changing the point of view. Let's see what this means.

Deep learning is applauded as an innovative approach among researchers and technical experts of AI, but the world in general doesn't know much about its greatness yet. Rather, they pay attention to what a machine can't do. For example, people don't really focus on the image recognition capabilities of MNIST using CNN, which generates a lower error rate than humans, but they criticize that a machine can't recognize images perfectly. This is probably because people expect a lot when they hear and imagine AI. We might need to change this mindset. Let's consider DORAEMON, a Japanese national cartoon character who is also famous worldwide—a robot who has high intelligence and AI, but often makes silly mistakes. Do we criticize him? No, we just laugh it off or take it as a joke and don't get serious. Also, think about DUMMY / DUM-E, the robot arm in the movie *Iron Man*. It has AI as well, but makes silly mistakes. See, they make mistakes but we still like them.

In this way, it might be better to emphasize the point that machines make mistakes. Changing the expression part of a user interface could be the trigger for people to adopt AI rather than just studying an algorithm the most. Who knows? It's highly likely that you can gain the world's interest by thinking of ideas in creative fields, not from the perspective of precision. Deep Dream by Google is one good example. We can do more exciting things when art or design and deep learning collaborate.

Summary

In this chapter, you learned how to utilize deep learning algorithms for practical applications. The fields that are well studied are image recognition and NLP. While learning about the field of NLP, we looked through two new deep learning models: the RNN and LSTM networks, which can be trained with time sequential data. The training algorithm used in these models is BPTT. You also learned that there are three approaches to make the best of the deep learning ability: the field-oriented approach, the breakdown-oriented approach, and the output-oriented approach. Each approach has a different angle, and can maximize the possibility for deep learning.

And …congratulations! You've just accomplished the learning part of deep learning with Java. Although there are still some models that have not been mentioned yet in this book, you can be sure there will be no problem in acquiring and utilizing them. The next chapter will introduce some libraries that are implemented with other programming languages, so just relax and take a look.

7

Other Important Deep Learning Libraries

In this chapter, we'll talk about other deep learning libraries, especially libraries with programming languages other than Java. The following are the most famous, well-developed libraries:

- Theano
- TensorFlow
- Caffe

You'll briefly learn about each of them. Since we'll mainly implement them using Python here, you can skip this chapter if you are not a Python developer. All the libraries introduced in this chapter support GPU implementations and have other special features, so let's dig into them.

Theano

Theano was developed for deep learning, but it is not actually a deep learning library; it is a Python library for scientific computing. The documentation is available at `http://deeplearning.net/software/theano/`. There are several characteristics introduced on the page such as the use of a GPU, but the most striking feature is that Theano supports **computational differentiation** or **automatic differentiation**, which ND4J, the Java scientific computing library, doesn't support. This means that, with Theano, we don't have to calculate the gradients of model parameters by ourselves. Theano automatically does this instead. Since Theano undertakes the most complicated parts of the algorithm, implementations of math expressions can be less difficult.

Let's see how Theano computes gradients. To begin with, we need to install Theano on the machine. Installation can be done just by using `pip install Theano` or `easy_install Theano`. Then, the following are the lines to import and use Theano:

```
import theano
import theano.tensor as T
```

With Theano, all variables are processed as tensors. For example, we have `scalar`, `vector`, and `matrix`, `d` for double, `l` for long, and so on. Generic functions such as `sin`, `cos`, `log`, and `exp` are also defined under `theano.tensor`. Therefore, as shown previously, we often use the alias of tensor, `T`.

As a first step to briefly grasp Theano implementations, consider the very simple parabola curve. The implementation is saved in `DLWJ/src/resources/theano/1_1_parabola_scalar.py` so that you can reference it. First, we define `x` as follows:

```
x = T.dscalar('x')
```

This definition is unique with Python because `x` doesn't have a value; it's just a symbol. In this case, `x` is `scalar` of the type `d` (double). Then we can define `y` and its gradient very intuitively. The implementation is as follows:

```
y = x ** 2
dy = T.grad(y, x)
```

So, `dy` should have `2x` within it. Let's check whether we can get the correct answers. What we need to do additionally is to register the `math` function with Theano:

```
f = theano.function([x], dy)
```

Then you can easily compute the value of the gradients:

```
print f(1)   # => 2.0
print f(2)   # => 4.0
```

Very simple! This is the power of Theano. We have `x` of scalar here, but you can easily implement vector (and matrix) calculations as well just by defining `x` as:

```
x = T.dvector('x')
y = T.sum(x ** 2)
```

We won't go further here, but you can find the completed codes in `DLWJ/src/resources/theano/1_2_parabola_vector.py` and `DLWJ/src/resources/theano/1_3_parabola_matrix.py`.

When we consider implementing deep learning algorithms with Theano, we can find some very good examples on GitHub in *Deep Learning Tutorials* (https://github.com/lisa-lab/DeepLearningTutorials). In this chapter, we'll look at an overview of the standard MLP implementation so you understand more about Theano. The forked repository as a snapshot is available at https://github.com/yusugomori/DeepLearningTutorials. First, let's take a look at mlp.py. The model parameters of the hidden layer are the weight and bias:

```
W = theano.shared(value=W_values, name='W', borrow=True)
b = theano.shared(value=b_values, name='b', borrow=True)
```

Both parameters are defined using theano.shared so that they can be accessed and updated through the model. The activation can be represented as follows:

$$z = h(Wx + b)$$

This denotes the activation function, that is, the hyperbolic tangent in this code. Therefore, the corresponding code is written as follows:

```
lin_output = T.dot(input, self.W) + self.b
self.output = (
    lin_output if activation is None
    else activation(lin_output)
)
```

Here, linear activation is also supported. Likewise, parameters w and b of the output layer, that is, logistic regression layer, are defined and initialized in logistic_sgd.py:

```
self.W = theano.shared(
    value=numpy.zeros(
        (n_in, n_out),
        dtype=theano.config.floatX
    ),
    name='W',
    borrow=True
)

self.b = theano.shared(
    value=numpy.zeros(
        (n_out,),
```

```
        dtype=theano.config.floatX
    ),
    name='b',
    borrow=True
)
```

The activation function of multi-class logistic regression is the `softmax` function and we can just write and define the output as follows:

```
self.p_y_given_x = T.nnet.softmax(T.dot(input, self.W) + self.b)
```

We can write the predicted values as:

```
self.y_pred = T.argmax(self.p_y_given_x, axis=1)
```

In terms of training, since the equations of the backpropagation algorithm are computed from the loss function and its gradient, what we need to do is just define the function to be minimized, that is, the negative log likelihood function:

```
def negative_log_likelihood(self, y):
    return -T.mean(T.log(self.p_y_given_x)[T.arange(y.shape[0]),
y])
```

Here, the mean values, not the sum, are computed to evaluate across the mini-batch.

With these preceding values and definitions, we can implement MLP. Here again, what we need to do is define the equations and symbols of MLP. The following is an extraction of the code:

```
class MLP(object):
    def __init__(self, rng, input, n_in, n_hidden, n_out):
        # self.hiddenLayer = HiddenLayer(...)
        # self.logRegressionLayer = LogisticRegression(...)

        # L1 norm
        self.L1 = (
            abs(self.hiddenLayer.W).sum()
            + abs(self.logRegressionLayer.W).sum()
        )

        # square of L2 norm
        self.L2_sqr = (
            (self.hiddenLayer.W ** 2).sum()
            + (self.logRegressionLayer.W ** 2).sum()
        )

        # negative log likelihood of MLP
```

```
self.negative_log_likelihood = (
    self.logRegressionLayer.negative_log_likelihood
)

# the parameters of the model
self.params = self.hiddenLayer.params +
self.logRegressionLayer.params
```

Then you can build and train the model. Let's look at the code in `test_mlp()`. Once you load the dataset and construct MLP, you can evaluate the model by defining the cost:

```
cost = (
    classifier.negative_log_likelihood(y)
    + L1_reg * classifier.L1
    + L2_reg * classifier.L2_sqr
)
```

With this cost, we get the gradients of the model parameters with just a single line of code:

```
gparams = [T.grad(cost, param) for param in classifier.params]
```

The following is the equation to update the parameters:

```
updates = [
    (param, param - learning_rate * gparam)
    for param, gparam in zip(classifier.params, gparams)
]
```

The code in the first bracket follows this equation:

$$\theta \leftarrow \theta - \eta \frac{\partial L}{\partial \theta}$$

Then, finally, we define the actual function for the training:

```
train_model = theano.function(
    inputs=[index],
    outputs=cost,
    updates=updates,
    givens={
        x: train_set_x[index * batch_size: (index + 1) *
        batch_size],
        y: train_set_y[index * batch_size: (index + 1) *
        batch_size]
    }
)
```

Each indexed input and label corresponds to x, y in *givens*, so when `index` is given, the parameters are updated with `updates`. Therefore, we can train the model with iterations of training epochs and mini-batches:

```
while (epoch < n_epochs) and (not done_looping):
    epoch = epoch + 1
        for minibatch_index in xrange(n_train_batches):
            minibatch_avg_cost = train_model(minibatch_index)
```

The original code has the test and validation part, but what we just mentioned is the rudimentary structure. With Theano, equations of gradients will no longer be derived.

TensorFlow

TensorFlow is the library for machine learning and deep learning developed by Google. The project page is `https://www.tensorflow.org/` and all the code is open to the public on GitHub at `https://github.com/tensorflow/tensorflow`. TensorFlow itself is written with C++, but it provides a Python and C++ API. We focus on Python implementations in this book. The installation can be done with `pip`, `virtualenv`, or `docker`. The installation guide is available at `https://www. tensorflow.org/versions/master/get_started/os_setup.html`. After the installation, you can import and use TensorFlow by writing the following code:

```
import tensorflow as tf
```

TensorFlow recommends you implement deep learning code with the following three parts:

- `inference()`: This makes predictions using the given data, which defines the model structure
- `loss()`: This returns the error values to be optimized
- `training()`: This applies the actual training algorithms by computing gradients

We'll follow this guideline. A tutorial on MNIST classifications for beginners is introduced on `https://www.tensorflow.org/versions/master/tutorials/ mnist/beginners/index.html` and the code for this tutorial can be found in `DLWJ/src/resources/tensorflow/1_1_mnist_simple.py`. Here, we consider refining the code introduced in the tutorial. You can see all the code in `DLWJ/src/ resources/tensorflow/1_2_mnist.py`.

First, what we have to consider is fetching the MNIST data. Thankfully, TensorFlow also provides the code to fetch the data in `https://github.com/tensorflow/tensorflow/blob/master/tensorflow/examples/tutorials/mnist/input_data.py` and we put the code into the same directory. Then, by writing the following code, you can import the MNIST data:

```
import input_data
```

MNIST data can be imported using the following code:

```
mnist = input_data.read_data_sets("MNIST_data/", one_hot=True)
```

Similar to Theano, we define the variable with no actual values as the placeholder:

```
x_placeholder = tf.placeholder("float", [None, 784])
label_placeholder = tf.placeholder("float", [None, 10])
```

Here, 784 is the number of units in the input layer and 10 is the number in the output layer. We do this because the values in the placeholder change in accordance with the mini-batches. Once you define the placeholder you can move on to the model building and training. We set the non-linear activation with the `softmax` function in `inference()` here:

```
def inference(x_placeholder):

    W = tf.Variable(tf.zeros([784, 10]))
    b = tf.Variable(tf.zeros([10]))

    y = tf.nn.softmax(tf.matmul(x_placeholder, W) + b)

    return y
```

Here, `W` and `b` are the parameters of the model. The `loss` function, that is, the `cross_entropy` function, is defined in `loss()` as follows:

```
def loss(y, label_placeholder):
    cross_entropy = - tf.reduce_sum(label_placeholder * tf.log(y))

    return cross_entropy
```

With the definition of `inference()` and `loss()`, we can train the model by writing the following code:

```
def training(loss):
    train_step =
    tf.train.GradientDescentOptimizer(0.01).minimize(loss)

    return train_step
```

GradientDescentOptimizer() applies the gradient descent algorithm. But be careful, as this method just defines the method of training and the actual training has not yet been executed. TensorFlow also supports AdagradOptimizer(), MemontumOptimizer(), and other major optimizing algorithms.

The code and methods explained previously are to define the model. To execute the actual training, you need to initialize a session of TensorFlow:

```
init = tf.initialize_all_variables()
sess.run(init)
```

Then we train the model with mini-batches. All the data in a mini-batch is stored in feed_dict and then used in sess.run():

```
for i in range(1000):
    batch_xs, batch_ys = mnist.train.next_batch(100)
    feed_dict = {x_placeholder: batch_xs, label_placeholder:
    batch_ys}

    sess.run(train_step, feed_dict=feed_dict)
```

That's it for the model training. It's very simple, isn't it? You can show the result by writing the following code:

```
def res(y, label_placeholder, feed_dict):
    correct_prediction = tf.equal(
        tf.argmax(y, 1), tf.argmax(label_placeholder, 1)
    )

    accuracy = tf.reduce_mean(
        tf.cast(correct_prediction, "float")
    )

    print sess.run(accuracy, feed_dict=feed_dict)
```

TensorFlow makes it super easy to implement deep learning and it is very useful. Furthermore, TensorFlow has another powerful feature, TensorBoard, to visualize deep learning. By adding a few lines of code to the previous code snippet, we can use this useful feature.

Let's see how the model is visualized first. The code is in DLWJ/src/resources/tensorflow/1_3_mnist_TensorBoard.py, so simply run it. After you run the program, type the following command:

```
$ tensorboard --logdir=<ABOSOLUTE_PATH>/data
```

Here, <ABSOLUTE_PATH> is the absolute path of the program. Then, if you access http://localhost:6006/ in your browser, you can see the following page:

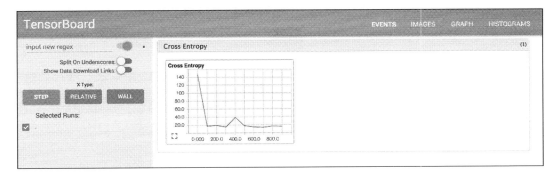

This shows the process of the value of cross_entropy. Also, when you click **GRAPH** in the header menu, you see the visualization of the model:

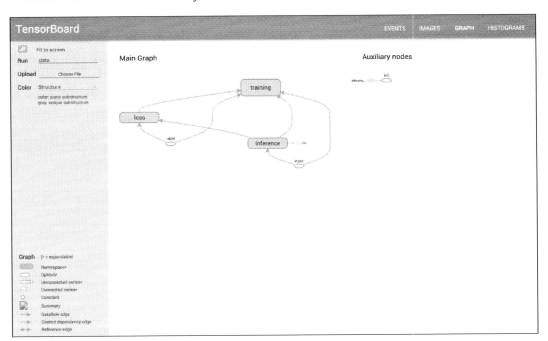

When you click on **inference** on the page, you can see the model structure:

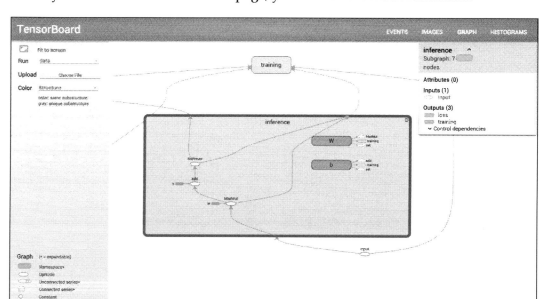

Now let's look inside the code. To enable visualization, you need to wrap the whole area with the scope: *with* tf.Graph().as_default(). By adding this scope, all the variables declared in the scope will be displayed in the graph. The displayed name can be set by including the name label as follows:

```
x_placeholder = tf.placeholder("float", [None, 784], name="input")
label_placeholder = tf.placeholder("float", [None, 10],
name="label")
```

Defining other scopes will create nodes in the graph and this is where the division, inference(), loss(), and training() reveal their real values. You can define the respective scope without losing any readability:

```
def inference(x_placeholder):
    with tf.name_scope('inference') as scope:
        W = tf.Variable(tf.zeros([784, 10]), name="W")
        b = tf.Variable(tf.zeros([10]), name="b")

        y = tf.nn.softmax(tf.matmul(x_placeholder, W) + b)
```

```
        return y

def loss(y, label_placeholder):
    with tf.name_scope('loss') as scope:
        cross_entropy = - tf.reduce_sum(label_placeholder *
        tf.log(y))

        tf.scalar_summary("Cross Entropy", cross_entropy)

    return cross_entropy

def training(loss):
    with tf.name_scope('training') as scope:
        train_step =
        tf.train.GradientDescentOptimizer(0.01).minimize(loss)

    return train_step
```

`tf.scalar_summary()` in `loss()` makes the variable show up in the **EVENTS** menu. To enable visualization, we need the following code:

```
summary_step = tf.merge_all_summaries()
init = tf.initialize_all_variables()

summary_writer = tf.train.SummaryWriter('data',
graph_def=sess.graph_def)
```

Then the process of variables can be added with the following code:

```
summary = sess.run(summary_step, feed_dict=feed_dict)
summary_writer.add_summary(summary, i)
```

This feature of visualization will be much more useful when we're using more complicated models.

Caffe

Caffe is a library famous for its speed. The official project page is http://caffe.berkeleyvision.org/ and the GitHub page is https://github.com/BVLC/caffe. Similar to TensorFlow, Caffe has been developed mainly with C++, but it provides a Python and MATLAB API. In addition, what is unique to Caffe is that you don't need any programming experience, you just write the configuration or protocol files, that is `.prototxt` files, to perform experiments and research with deep learning. Here, we focus on the protocol-based approach.

Caffe is a very powerful library that enables quick model building, training, and testing; however, it's a bit difficult to install the library to get a lot of benefits from it. As you can see from the installation guide at `http://caffe.berkeleyvision.org/installation.html`, you need to install the following in advance:

- CUDA
- BLAS (ATLAS, MKL, or OpenBLAS)
- OpenCV
- Boost
- Others: snappy, leveldb, gflags, glog, szip, lmdb, protobuf, and hdf5

Then, clone the repository from the GitHub page and create the `Makefile.config` file from `Makefile.config.example`. You may need Anaconda, a Python distribution, beforehand to run the `make` command. You can download this from `https://www.continuum.io/downloads`. After you run the `make`, `make test`, and `make runtest` commands (you may want to run the commands with a `-jN` option such as `make -j4` or `make -j8` to speed up the process) and pass the test, you'll see the power of Caffe. So, let's look at an example. Go to `$CAFFE_ROOT`, the path where you cloned the repository, and type the following commands:

```
$ ./data/mnist/get_mnist.sh
$ ./examples/mnist/train_lenet.sh
```

That's all you need to solve the standard MNIST classification problem with CNN. So, what happened here? When you have a look at `train_lenet.sh`, you will see the following:

```
#!/usr/bin/env sh

./build/tools/caffe train --solver=examples/mnist/lenet_solver.
prototxt
```

It simply runs the `caffe` command with the protocol file `lenet_solver.prototxt`. This file configures the hyper parameters of the model such as the learning rate and the momentum. The file also references the network configuration file, in this case, `lenet_train_test.prototxt`. You can define each layer with a JSON-like description:

```
layer {
  name: "conv1"
  type: "Convolution"
  bottom: "data"
  top: "conv1"
  param {
    lr_mult: 1
  }
  param {
    lr_mult: 2
  }
  convolution_param {
    num_output: 20
    kernel_size: 5
    stride: 1
    weight_filler {
      type: "xavier"
    }
    bias_filler {
      type: "constant"
    }
  }
}
```

So, basically, the protocol file is divided into two parts:

- **Net**: This defines the detailed structure of the model and gives a description of each layer, hence whole neural networks
- **Solver**: This defines the optimization settings such as the use of a CPU/GPU, the number of iterations, and the hyper parameters of the model such as the learning rate

Caffe can be a great tool when you need to apply deep learning to a large dataset with principal approaches.

Summary

In this chapter, you learned how to implement deep learning algorithms and models using Theano, TensorFlow, and Caffe. All of them have special and powerful features and each of them is very useful. If you are interested in other libraries and frameworks, you can have *Chainer* (http://chainer.org/), *Torch* (http://torch.ch/), *Pylearn2* (http://deeplearning.net/software/pylearn2/), *Nervana* (http://neon.nervanasys.com/), and so on. You can also reference some benchmark tests (https://github.com/soumith/convnet-benchmarks and https://github.com/soumith/convnet-benchmarks/issues/66) when you actually consider building your application with one of the libraries mentioned earlier.

Throughout this book, you learned the fundamental theories and algorithms of machine learning and deep learning and how deep learning is applied to study/business fields. With the knowledge and techniques you've acquired here, you should be able to cope with any problems that confront you. While it is true that you still need more steps to realize AI, you now have the greatest opportunity to achieve innovation.

8

What's Next?

In the previous chapters, we learned the concept, theory, implementation of deep learning, and how to use libraries. Now you know the basic technique of deep learning, so don't worry. On the other hand, development of deep learning is rapid and a new model might be developed tomorrow. Big news about AI or deep learning comes out one after the other every day. Since you have acquired the basic technique, you can learn about the upcoming new technologies on AI and deep learning quickly. Now, let's walk away from the details of techniques and think about what path the field of AI will or should take. What is the future of deep learning? For the closing chapter, let's think about that. We'll pick up the following topics in this chapter:

- Hot topics in the deep learning industry
- How to manage AI technologies
- How to proceed the study of deep learning further

As for the last topic, about further study, I will recommend a website about deep learning. You can stay ahead of the curve by thinking about what technology might come next, or leveraging the techniques you have learned to innovate, rather than following AI developments as they appear.

Breaking news about deep learning

Deep learning, which triggered the AI boom, can't stop its momentum. New results are reported each day. As mentioned in *Chapter 6, Approaches to Practical Applications – Recurrent Neural Networks and More*, many researchers compete on image recognition and natural language processing. Of course, deep learning is not limited to these two fields, but applies to many other fields. The outcome of these applications is very exciting.

In this AI boom, in March 2016, the Go world was shaken by one event. Go is a board game in which two players are trying to take over more territory than their opponent. The news of 'AI beating a human in Go' shocked not only Go players but also the whole world, when a machine, that is, AI, beat a human at Go. DeepMind (`https://deepmind.com/`), which was bought by Google, has been developing the Go-playing AI, called AlphaGo, and AlphaGo has beaten world-class player Lee Sedol for a fourth time, to win the five-game series four games to one in Google's DeepMind Challenge Match. Each game was delivered on livestream via YouTube, and many people watched the games in real time. You can watch all five games on YouTube, if you haven't watched them yet:

- **Match 1**: `https://www.youtube.com/watch?v=vFr3K2DORc8`
- **Match 2**: `https://www.youtube.com/watch?v=l-GsfyVCBu0`
- **Match 3**: `https://www.youtube.com/watch?v=qUAmTYHEyM8`
- **Match 4**: `https://www.youtube.com/watch?v=yCALyQRN3hw`
- **Match 5**: `https://www.youtube.com/watch?v=mzpW10DPHeQ`

In these games, the first match, Match 1, gained a particularly large amount of attention. Also, looking at the number of page views, which is more than 1.35 million, you can see that many people have watched the video of Match 4, which was the only match that AlphaGo lost to Lee Se-Dol. The following is an image which captured one scene of Match 1:

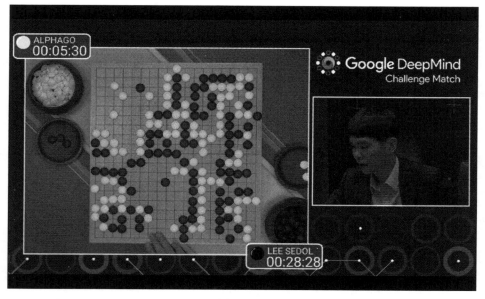

The moment AlphaGo beat Lee SeDol (`https://www.youtube.com/watch?v=vFr3K2DORc8`)

That was the moment at which not only researchers of AI, but also the world, were excited by AlphaGo; but why did this news got so much attention? For another board game example, in a chess match, Deep Blue, which was developed by IBM, beat the world chess champion in 1997. Of course, it became big news at that time, as this was also a moment when a machine beat a human. Why then, when this was not the first time a machine had beaten a human, was news of AlphaGo's triumph against Lee SeDol so world-shaking? What is the difference between Chess and Go? Well, the difference is in the complexity of the patterns of Go. In fact, Go has many more strategy patterns than Chess. In popular board games such as Chess, Shogi, and Go, the numbers of patterns to determine who wins or loses are as follows:

- Chess: 10,120
- Shogi: 10,220
- Go: 10,360

Even looking at the numbers, you can see how complicated the strategy of Go is and easily imagine that a machine also needs an enormous amount of calculation. Because of this huge number of patterns, until recently, people thought it was impossible for AlphaGo to beat a human, or that it would be 100 years or 200 years before AlphaGo would beat a human. It was considered impossible for a machine to calculate the patterns of Go within a realistic time. But now, in a matter of a few years, a machine has beaten a human. According to the Google research blog, 1.5 months before the DeepMind Challenge Match was held, DeepMind could predict the human's moves 57% of the time (`http://googleresearch.blogspot.jp/2016/01/alphago-mastering-ancient-game-of-go.html`). The fact that a machine won against a human definitely had an impact, but the fact that a machine could learn the strategy of Go within a realistic time was even more surprising. DeepMind applies deep neural networks with the combination of Monte Carlo tree search and reinforcement learning, which shows the width of the application range for the algorithm of deep neural networks.

Expected next actions

Since the news about AlphaGo was featured in the media, the AI boom has definitely had a boost. You might notice that you hear the words "deep learning" in the media more often recently. It can be said that the world's expectations of AI have been increased that much. What is interesting is that the term "deep learning," which was originally a technical term, is now used commonly in daily news. You can see that the image of the term **AI** has been changing. Probably, until just a few years ago, if people heard about AI, many of them would have imagined an actual robot, but how about now? The term AI is now often used — not particularly consciously — with regard to software or applications, and is accepted as commonplace. This is nothing but an indication that the world has started to understand AI, which has been developed for research, correctly. If a technology is taken in the wrong direction, it generates repulsion, or some people start to develop the technology incorrectly; however, it seems that this boom in AI technology is going in a good direction so far.

While we are excited about the development of AI, as a matter of course, some people feel certain fears or anxieties. It's easy to imagine that some people might think the world where machines dominate humans, like in sci-fi movies or novels, is coming sooner or later, especially after AlphaGo won over Lee SeDol in the Go world, where it was said to be impossible for a machine to beat a human; the number of people who feel anxious might increase. However, although the news that a machine has beaten a human could be taken as a negative if you just focus on the fact that "a machine won," this is definitely not negative news. Rather, it is great news for humankind. Why? Here are two reasons.

The first reason is that the Google DeepMind Challenge Match was a match in which the human was handicapped. Not only for Go, but also for card games or sports games, we usually do research about what tactics the opponents will use before a match, building our own strategy by studying opponents' action patterns. DeepMind, of course, has studied professional Go players' tactics and how to play, whereas humans couldn't study enough about how a machine plays, as DeepMind continued studying and kept changing its action patterns until the last minutes before the Google DeepMind Challenge Match. Therefore, it can be said that there was an information bias or handicap. It was great that Lee SeDol won one match with these handicaps. Also, it indicates that AI will develop further.

The other reason is that we have found that a machine is not likely to destroy the value of humans, but instead to promote humans' further growth. In the Google DeepMind Challenge Match, a machine used a strategy which a human had not used before. This fact was a huge surprise to us, but at the same time, it meant that we found a new thing which humans need to study. Deep learning is obviously a great technology, but we shouldn't forget that neural networks involve an algorithm which imitates the structure of a human brain. In other words, its fundamentals are the same as a human's patterns of thinking. A machine can find out an oversight of patterns which the human brain can't calculate by just adding the speed of calculation. AlphaGo can play a game against AlphaGo using the input study data, and learns from the result of that game too. Unlike a human, a machine can proceed to study for 24 hours, so it can gain new patterns rapidly. Then, a whole new pattern will be found by a machine during that process, which can be used for humans to study Go further. By studying a new strategy which wouldn't been found just by a human, our Go world will expand and we can enjoy Go even more. Needless to say, it is not only machines that learn, but also humans. In various fields, a machine will discover new things which a human hasn't ever noticed, and every time humans face that new discovery, they too advance.

AI and humans are in a complementary relationship. To reiterate, a machine is good at calculating huge numbers of patterns and finding out a pattern which hasn't been discovered yet. This is way beyond human capability. On the other hand, AI can't create a new idea from a completely new concept, at least for now. On the contrary, this is the area where humans excel. A machine can judge things only within given knowledge. For example, if AI is only given many kinds of dog images as input data, it can answer what kind of dog it is, but if it's a cat, then AI would try its best to answer the kind of dog, using its knowledge of dogs.

AI is actually an innocent existence in a way, and it just gives the most likely answer from its gained knowledge. Thinking what knowledge should be given for AI to make progress is a human's task. If you give new knowledge, again AI will calculate the most likely answer from the given knowledge with quite a fast pace. People also have different interests or knowledge depending on the environment in which they grow up, which is the same for AI. Meaning, what kind of *personality* the AI has or whether the AI becomes good or evil for humans depends on the person/people the AI has contact with. One such typical example, in which AI was grown in the wrong way, is the AI developed by Microsoft called Tay (`https://www.tay.ai`). On March 23, 2016, Tay appeared on Twitter with the following tweet: *helloooooo world!!!*

Tay gains knowledge from the interaction between users on Twitter and posts new tweets. This trial itself is quite interesting.

However, immediately after it was made open to the public, the problem occurred. On Twitter, users played a prank on Tay by inputting discriminatory knowledge into its account. Because of this, Tay has grown to keep posting tweets including expressions of sexual discrimination. And only one day after Tay appeared on Twitter, Tay disappeared from Twitter, leaving the following tweet: *c u soon humans need sleep now so many conversations today thx.*

If you visit Tay's Twitter account's page (`https://twitter.com/tayandyou`), tweets are protected and you can't see them anymore:

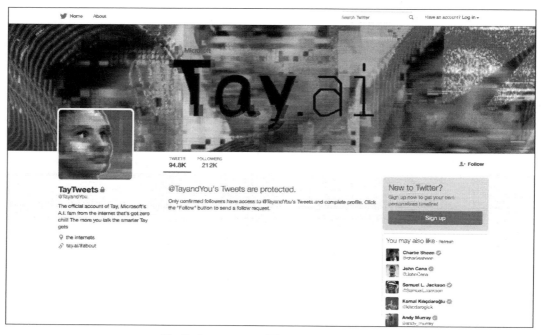

The Twitter account of Tay is currently closed

This is exactly the result of AI being given the wrong training by humans. In these past few years, the technology of AI has got huge attention, which can be one of the factors to speed up the development of AI technology further. Now, the next action that should be taken is to think how AI and humans interact with each other. AI itself is just one of many technologies. Technology can become good or evil depending on how humans use it; therefore, we should be careful how we control that technology, otherwise it's possible that the whole AI field will be shrinking in the future. AI is becoming particularly good within certain narrow fields, but it is far from overwhelming, and far from what science fiction currently envisions. How AI will evolve in the future depends on our use of knowledge and technology management.

While we should definitely care about how to control the technology, we can't slow down the speed of its development. Considering recent booms of bots, as seen in the story that Facebook is going to launch Bot Store (`http://techcrunch.com/2016/03/17/facebooks-messenger-in-a-bot-store/`), we can easily imagine that the interaction between a user and an application would become a chat-interface base, and AI would mingle with the daily life of an ordinary user going forward. For more people to get familiar with AI, we should develop AI technology further and make it more convenient for people to use.

Deep learning and AI have got more attention, which means that if you would like to produce an outstanding result in this field, you are likely to find fierce competition. It's highly likely that an experiment you would like to work on might already be being worked on by someone else. The field of deep learning is becoming a world of such high competition as start-ups. If you own huge data, you might take advantage by analyzing that data, but otherwise, you need to think about how to experiment with limited data. Still, if you would like to get outstanding performance, it might be better for you to always bear the following in mind:

 Deep learning can only judge things within the knowledge given by training.

Based on this, you might get an interesting result by taking the following two approaches:

- Experiment with data which can easily produce both input data and output data for training and testing
- Use completely different types of data, for training and test respectively, in an experiment

For the first approach, for example, you can check automatic colorization using CNN. It was introduced in the project open to the public online at `http://tinyclouds.org/colorize/` or in the dissertation at `http://arxiv.org/pdf/1603.08511v1.pdf`. The idea is to color gray-scale images automatically. If you have any colored images – these should be obtained very easily – you can generate grayscale images just by writing quick scripts. With that, you have now prepared input data and output data for training. Being able to prepare lots of data means you can test easier and get high precision more often. The following is one of the examples of the tests:

Both are cited from `http://tinyclouds.org/colorize/`

Inputs to the model are the grayscale images on the left, outputs are the middle, and the images on the right are the ones with true color.

For the second approach, using completely different types of data, for training and testing respectively, in an experiment, we intentionally provide data which the AI doesn't know and make the gap between a random answer and a correct answer interesting/fun. For example, in *Generating Stories about Images* (https://medium.com/@samim/generating-stories-about-images-d163ba41e4ed), they have provided an image of a sumo wrestler to neural networks, which have only studied one of the projects and introduces the following: romantic novels and then test what the neural networks think. The result is as follows:

Generated story about image
Model: Romantic Novels

"He was a shirtless man in the back of his mind, and I let out a curse as he leaned over to kiss me on the shoulder.

He wanted to strangle me, considering the beatiful boy I'd become wearing his boxers."

Cited from https://medium.com/@samim/generating-stories-about-images-d163ba41e4ed

This experiment itself is based on the approach called neural-storyteller (https://github.com/ryankiros/neural-storyteller), but since the given data has an idea, it got the interesting result. As such, adding your new idea to an already developed approach would be an approach which could also get an interesting result.

Useful news sources for deep learning

Well, lastly, let's pick up two websites which would be useful for watching the movement of deep learning going forward and for learning more and more new knowledge. It will help your study.

The first one is **GitXiv** (`http://gitxiv.com/`). The top page is as follows:

In GitXiv, there are mainly articles based on papers. But in addition to the links to papers, it sets the links to codes which were used for tests, hence you can shorten your research time. Of course, it updates new experiments one after another, so you can watch what approach is major or in which field deep learning is hot now. It sends the most updated information constantly if you register your e-mail address. You should try it:

The second one is **Deep Learning News** (`http://news.startup.ml/`). This is a collection of links for deep learning and machine learning related topics. It has the same UI as **Hacker News** (`https://news.ycombinator.com/`), which deals with news for the whole technology industry, so if you know Hacker News, you should be familiar with the layout:

The information on Deep Learning News is not updated that frequently, but it has tips not only for implementation or technique, but also tips for what field you can use for deep learning, and has deep learning and machine learning related event information, so it can be useful for ideation or inspiration. If you take a brief look at the URL in the top page list, you might come up with good ideas.

There are more useful websites, materials, and communities other than the two we picked up here, such as the deep learning group on Google+ (`https://plus.google.com/communities/112866381580457264725`), so you should watch the media which suit you. Anyway, now this industry is developing rapidly and it is definitely necessary to always watch out for updated information.

Summary

In this chapter, we went from the example of AlphaGo as breaking news to the consideration of how deep learning will or should develop. A machine winning over a human in some areas is not worthy of fear, but is an opportunity for humans to grow as well. On the other hand, it is quite possible that this great technology could go in the wrong direction, as seen in the example of Tay, if the technology of AI isn't handled appropriately. Therefore, we should be careful not to destroy this steadily developing technology.

The field of deep learning is one that has the potential for hugely changing an era with just one idea. If you build AI in the near future, that AI is, so to speak, a pure existence without any knowledge. Thinking what to teach AI, how to interact with it, and how to make use of AI for humankind is humans' work. You, as a reader of this book, will lead a new technology in the right direction. Lastly, I hope you will get actively involved in the cutting edge of the field of AI.

Index